OPALS

Text and Photographs
Fred Ward

Editing
Charlotte Ward

As with emeralds from Colombia and rubies from Burma, black opals from Australia define the world opal market. An American miner found this superb example in Lightning Ridge. With a classic harlequin pattern, the most desired and expensive, this beautiful specimen almost certainly found a home in Asia.

HISTORY
AND LORE

O pal—chameleon of a thousand colors...essence of every gem dis-
tilled into one...shimmering stone of love and hope...a gift delivered
from heaven in bolts of lightning...talisman of thieves and
spies...nature's fireworks...October's opulent jewel...the Queen of Gems. Do
all of these accolades refer to the same gemstone?

Yes, and so can many, many more, because opal generates the
strongest, most sensual emotions, as various as the colors it flashes. Great
beauty makes it the best known, most loved, most popular of all the
"phenomenal" gemstones—those that show unusual optical effects—the
gems that do tricks. The term *play-of-color* was created solely to describe opal's
shifting of spectral hues.

Precious opal is by definition opal with play-of-color. *Common opal*
refers to opal with no color play. Such opal is called *potch* in Australia,
although some Aussies insist that because of a random silica sphere arrange-
ment in potch, it is different from common opal. Internationally the terms are
used interchangeably, as they are in this book. Common opal occurs throughout the world in black, white, and a variety of colors, such as yellow, green,
blue, and pink. Some colored potch is sold for gem use. Mexican fire opal, an
orange to red variety, is considered gem material even without play-of-color.
Precious Mexican fire opal exhibits play-of-color on an orange-red field.

In a cave in Kenya, Louis Leakey, the famous anthropologist,
uncovered the earliest known opal artifacts. Dating back to about 4000 B.C.,
they most likely came from Ethiopia. Historically, opal discoveries and
mining progressed similarly to the ways diamond, emerald, ruby, and sapphire were produced. As early humans found various gemstones, they slowly
learned to work them into decorative shapes. As communities developed and
gems became symbols of wealth, people realized that prospecting for gem-

Shrouded in mystery, the **Hope Opal** *rests in obscurity compared to its
famous collection cousin, the* **Hope Diamond.** *Also called the* **Aztec Sun
God Opal,** *the 35-carat transparent blue gem with play-of-color,
features a carved human face surrounded by sun rays. Assumed to be
Mexican when catalogued in 1839, the opal's origin remains unknown.*

Even though some Kenyan opal artifacts date to 4000 B.C., most authorities agree that the Romans raised opal to gemstone status about 100 B.C. Most or all early Old World gem opal originated in an area that used to be in Hungary; the area is now part of the Slovak Republic (left). The Hungarian mines were Europe's opal source until the 1500s, when Spanish conquerors returned from the New World with opals from Mexico and the Andes. In the 1890s superior opals began arriving in great quantities from Australia's new mines, and the Hungarian mines gradually closed.

stones was more profitable and efficient than happily stumbling upon the occasional pickup. In the Old World, Hungary mined opal for Europe and the Middle East, while Mexico, Peru, and Honduras supplied their own native empires with the gemstone. Conquistadors introduced New World opal to Spain when they returned with stones in the early sixteenth century. Since the late 1800s Australia has dominated opal production with more than ninety percent of the global output. Opal of differing qualities occurs in more than twenty other countries, including Zambia, Ethiopia, Guatemala, Poland, Peru, Canada, New Zealand, and Indonesia. Besides Australia, the USA, Brazil, and Mexico produce reliable commercial supplies of gem opal.

Ancient Romans provided the first real market for opal. With a rich powerful empire, wealthy citizens acquired disposable income and a passion for gems. Opal, whose colors changed with every shift of light, was rarer than pearls and diamonds and destined to be the stuff of myths and dreams. The great Roman writer Pliny, whom I consider to be the world's first gemologist, tells the tale of the Roman senator Nonius, who in 50 B.C. flaunted his most prized possession, a ring featuring a brilliant opal about the size of a hazelnut. It so happened that the opal caught the eye of Mark Anthony, who is said to have coveted it for his paramour, Cleopatra. When Nonius refused an offer for the opal, Anthony responded with stern orders. Nonius fled for this life, banished from Rome forever.

Writing before his death in 79 A.D., Pliny described opal as second in value only to emeralds, having "a refulgent fire of the carbuncle (ruby or

In Australia's desolate outback, away from all conveniences and confronting a harsh and dangerous climate, early opal miners overcame great personal hardship in order to dig both light and black opals. They made arduous trips by foot, horseback, and camel-train to and from the mines.

Starting in 1896, Ernie Sherman (left, top) tried his hand at mining and bought opal from this White Cliffs house. Like Coober Pedy and Andamooka miners before him, Ernie's son Greg, a buyer since the 1940s, learned to escape 130°F-summer heat by living underground (left, bottom).

garnet), the glorious purple of amethyst, the sea green of emerald, and all those colors glittering together mixed in an incredible way." The opal Romans treasured almost certainly came from an area that initially was in Hungary, but Pliny thought it had originated in India. He had been deceived by dealers who probably had hoped to capitalize on the appeal of "oriental" imports. Believing opal to be the quintessence of all gems, Romans bought stones mined in a region that earlier this century was incorporated into Czechoslovakia. The area is now part of the Slovak Republic.

Still referred to as the Hungarian opal mines, they operated for more than two thousand years, until 1922, an extraordinary life span matched only by India's alluvial diamond fields and Egypt's emerald-producing Cleopatra's Mines. The entire time the Hungarian mines supplied Europe with opal, including a stone for the crown of a Holy Roman emperor, superstitions circulated attributing evil powers and maladies to the colorful stone. In the eleventh century, Bishop Marbode of Rennes wrote of opal "...Yet 'tis the guardian of the thievish race;/It gifts the bearer with acutest sight/But clouds all other eyes with thickest night." With those and three more hexameter lines, opal became known as the talisman of spies and robbers. There are a few folks who will believe anything!

Opals have sometimes been associated with bad luck. One royal opal did bring terrible misfortune to the hapless goldsmith who broke it during setting. The unforgiving Louis XI ordered his hands cut off. No surprise that few of his colleagues thereafter had anything good to tell buyers about opal.

Soon after Australia's opals appeared, European and American designers began producing gorgeous creations, such as this opal, diamond, and platinum brooch. The black opal was mined in Lightning Ridge around 1920.

Jayson Traurig Bros. of Australia

5

The saddest opal saga is the oft-repeated misconception in the last of Sir Walter Scott's novels, *Anne of Geierstein* (1829), which irrevocably linked opal to misfortune. Having not read the third volume, the public jumped to the conclusion that the heroine has been bewitched, that her magic opal discolors when touched by holy water, and that she dies as a result. On carefully examining the texts, Si Frazier, writing in *Lapidary Journal*, found all three accusations false. The opal, which actually belonged to Anne's exotic grandmother, loses its color through no malevolence. Quite the contrary, as Anne explains to her suitor, "...it is said to be the nature of that noble gem [to pale as a warning to its owner] on the approach of poison," the cause of her grandmother's death. Even so, this single work plunged opal prices to half in just one year and crippled the European opal market for decades.

The combination of Australia's massive opal discoveries and Queen Victoria's enthusiasm for the gem ultimately transformed the opal market. However, the introduction of Australia's opal still faced rough sailing. Until the late 1800s, Europeans had seen only Hungarian stones, which were usually white with little color play. Suddenly large, brilliant Australian opals appeared, dancing with fire. Suspecting fakes, British gem dealers had to be coaxed to buy the new gemstones. But Queen Victoria saved the day. Loving both Australia and its opal, she presented the new gems as gifts and included them as significant portions of her daughters' dowries. By the end of the 1890s, instead of being unlucky and "out," opal was favored, and "in."

Fabulous Australian opal began to appear during an eighty-year wave of discovery across the southern half of the awakening continent. Starting in 1849, white common opal was unearthed in South Australia. The first opal with play-of-color was found in Victoria during 1863, quickly followed by Queensland's opal. In 1890 Australia's first commercial opal mine exported large colorful light opal from White Cliffs in New South Wales. Stunning black opal out of Lightning Ridge beginning in 1903 made Australia the world's largest producer of the world's finest opal.

A year later South Australia yielded its first precious opal. And only a decade later, the enormous deposits at Coober Pedy altered the world perception of opal size and availability. Up the road a few hours, the strangely beautiful Mintabie field followed with its full range of black, dark, and light opal after 1921. The final major field, Andamooka, opened in 1930. By then, Australia owned the opal market. Considered a small player for most of its life, Mintabie grew quickly in the late 1970s with the introduction of heavy earth-moving equipment. It eclipsed its better-known neighbor, Coober Pedy, for two years in the 1980s to become the world's largest opal producer. To understand more of opal's past and its prospects, refer to the map to see where it occurs, and you probably can predict future opal discoveries.

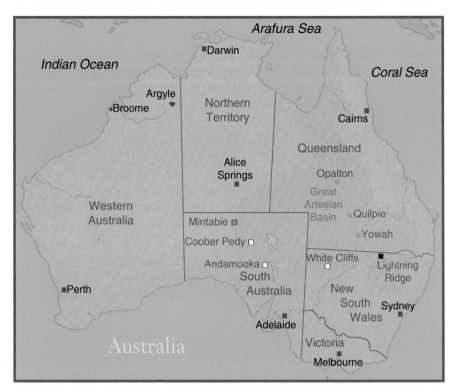

ustralia's famous opal mines, Mintabie, Coober Pedy, Andamooka, White Cliffs, and Lightning Ridge, form a gentle arc across a third of the country. Their locations are no accident. Observe the most significant feature of the map above, the teal-colored area known as the Great Artesian Basin. During the Jurassic and Cretaceous Periods, 70 to 200 million years ago, a huge shallow inland sea bathed the interior. Slowly, thick sandy sediments and sandy clay sediments settled over much of what is today Australia. In the Tertiary Period, 37 to 70 million years ago, the earth's climate changed, the sea receded, and the watery basin returned to desert. The top one hundred feet below today's ground level became layers of deposited gray shales, shaley mudstones, limestone, and sandstone.

Although there are several conflicting theories about opal formation and silica sources, most researchers believe that the majority of Australia's opal formed after Cretaceous sediments weathered, thus liberating silica. During heavy rainfalls the silica-rich water trickled through faults in the subsoil. Sometimes silica replaced buried wood, shell, or bone to form opal fossils (see pages 42-45). More often, either cavities or hard clay layers trapped the dissolved silica. As more silica descended with more water, which slowly evaporated, silica concentrated to the point where it agglomerated, forming microscopic spheres. A long steady rate of deposition and evaporation produced spheres of uniform size and shape, vital to the formation of precious opal (see pages 62-63). Irregularity in sphere size, shape, or alignment produced common opal.

Notice on the map that most famous opal mines are on or near the southern shore of the Great Artesian Basin. Vast sections of this ancient shoreline remain to be prospected for opal.

7

BLACK OPAL

Shakespeare understood the whimsical play-of-color that distinguishes opal. In *Twelfth Night* the clown observes of the Duke, who falls in love capriciously, "Now, the melancholy god protect thee; and the tailor make thy doublet of changeable taffeta, for thy mind is a very opal." But the Duke couples Olivia, the object of his passion, with the beautiful stone, alluding to both as the "queen of gems." If opal is queen, then black opal is without doubt king of opal, nature's presentation stone, complete with a velvety background upon which a dazzling foreground performs rippling color changes.

The opal trade has traditionally used *black*, *semi-black*, and *white* to distinguish the main varieties, too few steps to deal with the many nuances of opal. The Australian Gemstone Industry Council now proposes renaming these three *black*, *dark*, and *light*. On a neutral (colorless) scale based on the GSA Munsell Rock Color Chart, the Australians want to designate the four darkest body tones, N1-N4, as *black opal*; grades N5-N6 as *dark opal*; and N7-N9 as *light opal*. N9 could also be called *white opal*. As the Australian opal industry introduces its plan, buyers should realize what the report calls *body colour* is what most of us know as *body tone*, the relative darkness or lightness remaining once you disregard body color (hue) and play-of-color. Unlike black pearls, black sapphires, or black diamonds, black opals are not entirely black. The *black* in *black opal* means the gem has a very dark body tone.

Black opal is the most coveted of all opal varieties, and, at the high end of the market, the most expensive by far. Few great black opals ever reach USA dealers; instead they sell mainly in Japan. Though individual gems can fetch $100,000 to $500,000 or more today, at the turn of the century even spectacular examples of the then-new black opal were considered worthless.

The first Europeans to see black opal were a few ranchers who lived in Lightning Ridge around 1900. The area, about seven hundred kilometers northwest of Sydney on the northern border of New South Wales, was grazing land. The only commercial opal activity was another eight hundred kilometers southwest into the bush, at White Cliffs, a light opal mine.

Solid Precious Opal →   ← Precious Opal

← Potch

Intense colors characterize black opal (opposite), which can be all precious opal or opal cut to include dark potch (see cross-sections above). In these most expensive of all opals, **black** *refers to body tone when viewed face up.*

Lightning Ridge, home of Australia's black opal, prides itself on isolation and rugged individualism, as illustrated by its disdain of a census (left). The best estimate is about 15,000 people call "the Ridge" home, only 1800 of which have registered to vote.

An ideal place to get lost, the Ridge requires hard work and infinite optimism, a place where a van that should have been scrapped, flies. From the air Lightning Ridge looks deserted because most people work underground (right).

Gold miner Charlie Nettleton wandered into the Cliffs as the mine was slowing down. He tried opal, but had no luck. Undeterred and hearing of gold finds to the east, Charlie set out again, this time walking several hundred kilometers during the summer of 1901-1902, the hottest anyone could remember. On his way through Lightning Ridge heading north to look for gold, he camped with a local family, the Ryans, who showed him brilliant opal unlike any he had ever seen. So Charlie decided to pursue their line of work. He sank his first opal shaft in 1902, but nothing came of it. Then he moved close to where seven other men were digging, and here in early 1903, he struck opal. Charlie collected enough of the beautiful new material to send a parcel to a Sydney gem dealer.

Poor Charlie. For all that work, the dealer offered a dollar for his bagful, calling it "a worthless form of matrix." But opal miners are a steely lot. Rejecting the offer, Charlie spent the rest of 1903 walking from Lightning Ridge back to White Cliffs. Undaunted, he sought out a field buyer for T.C. Wollaston, whom Ridge historian Len Cram calls the "greatest opal merchant of all time." Although Charlie sold his first bag of black opal for only A£15, Wollaston placed a standing order for all he could mine. Lightning Ridge might have folded in 1903. Instead, from one humble sale, the Ridge grew to be the most important opal field in the world.

I have visited hundreds of gem mines on six continents over the past two decades, yet never have I seen another mine like Lightning Ridge. Life on the Ridge is still raw, the most obvious comparison being with America's Wild West in the late 1800s—a hideaway for loners, a place for getting lost. In fact, I suspect that the vast majority of its miners first came to the Ridge to escape—something or someone— and stayed to dig opal. Folks go by their first names—or aliases— keep no records, and guard information. Opal is an all-cash business, an on-the-spot done-deal, settled with a pile of A$50 or A$100 bills and no paperwork. Recently, a Midwest attorney representing a USA gem dealer asked me to help convince the

Internal Revenue Service that big-bill cash payments are the Australian norm and that his client could never produce receipts. I recounted the afternoon an old Ridge miner sat at a card table filled with his expensive opals and a prospective buyer's stack of fresh money. Explaining the payment system, the miner observed dryly, "Nothing ever goes wrong with a $100 bill."

Ratting," or stealing opal from somebody else's claim, is the most serious mine crime by far. Miners seldom report ratting, but they do police themselves privately, quickly, and efficiently. As one miner explained, a ratter can steal A$250,000 of opal in one night but be charged by the authorities only for trespassing. There may be some law on the Ridge that comes into play when absolutely necessary; however, frontier justice seems to serve. Victimized miners fire-bombed one known ratter's house three times before the thief got the message and fled town. Drive-by shootings are usually the second warning for such infractions; firing after aiming comes next. There are a lot of abandoned shafts at every mine site.

The most entertaining ratting story I have ever heard took place in a mine I was visiting. The pair of owners were "on opal." Having made a substantial find, they had been working feverishly to dig out their gems, but a ratter kept sneaking in after dark to steal all he could before daylight. Exasperated, one partner flew to Sydney to buy a dye bomb, such as bank tellers toss into bags to mark money after a robbery. Having rigged the bomb, the miners went to bed. About midnight they heard an explosion and scrambled down to find the mine shaft covered with fluorescent blue paint. Next morning at the Lightning Ridge police station, a low-life showed up demanding to swear out an arrest warrant. He accused the two miners of assault and battery, as well as endanger-

E. Gregory Sherman, Pty. Ltd.

ing his life. When the police sergeant stopped laughing, he took a long look at the bright blue ratter, stared him straight in the eye, and bellowed in his best Aussie legalese, "Piss off!"

Australian opal mining has to be the freest, most chaotic, least controlled in the world—the ultimate in laissez-faire enterprise. Although the country has a reputation for stringent immigration laws and work permits for foreigners, with opal mining, anything goes. As astounding as it may seem, anyone who can make it to an opal field can file for any piece of land not already claimed and being worked. For A$175 (A$100 bond, A$25 compensation, A$50 registration) and A$50 renewal annually, you can stake a claim 50 x 50 meters. It is yours as long as you pay the renewal fee on time and work the claim. All you find is yours, what you sell goes for cash, and when you want to leave, you can walk away without filling in shafts or tunnels or even covering the holes (only losing your A$100 bond). Backfilling is the law, but weaving among a vast number of abandoned open shafts at Lightning Ridge and Coober Pedy, I clearly noticed a gap in the enforcement system.

Opal mining rule one: Dig near someone who has already found opal. Short of moving next door to success, with so much land available, miners develop individual systems for choosing sites. As there is no reason to stay on unproductive ground, miners work multiple claims over the years. Now that people have tramped the Ridge for almost a century, they have already picked up most of the *floaters*, loose opals on the surface. Today's typical method for prospecting a new site involves searching for slips, or joints, vertical openings that originally admitted groundwater. Miners use the tried-and-true method of their predecessors—dousing. Walking the surface like well-diggers, they loosely hold two metal divining rods parallel. The rods swing together or apart in response to underground water. Once miners mark the joints, they stake a claim.

To be profitable with open cast, or surface mining, opal deposits have to be shallow or distributed randomly at all levels. Boulder opal miners in Queensland dig to shallow levels. At Mintabie, miners bulldoze to 100 feet

Some miners prefer handwork in order to lower costs and reduce breakage. Peter Cinar alone dug this warren of tunnels (right). His compensation, a personal treasure, was an eagle "picture opal."

Mining equipment is common at Lightning Ridge today. Operating 30-60 feet below the surface requires lowering the machine parts and reassembling the digger underground. Once the miner uncovers an opal seam, he carefully proceeds to dig with jackhammers and picks.

because opals occur randomly. But at Lightning Ridge, Coober Pedy, and Andamooka, with seam opal, miners still work underground.

After miners stake their claim and secure funding, they sink a 40-foot or more shaft and tunnel away from it. Twenty-five years ago they dug all shafts and tunnels by hand. Now they employ an auger, a giant drill, to open a circular shaft in hours. Once on the bottom, miners begin working their claims with a variety of mining gear designed to help them move dirt so they can look for opal. They lower partially disassembled Bobcats, or similar diggers, and reassemble them in the "gallery," where tunnels come together at the shaft. Unlike smaller hand-dug operations at both Coober Pedy and Mintabie, black opal mines have such huge profit potential that most operations can afford heavy equipment, making it possible to complete mining a claim in a fraction of the time it would have taken to hand dig.

Miners do not file accurate tunnel maps or, truth be told, know exactly where they will dig tomorrow. When "on opal," they follow gem seams, no matter what. Although claims are granted in either 50- or 100-meter lengths, no surveys keep miners within their underground boundaries. Danger arises because no one knows how near others are digging or where they have set explosives. Also, it is impossible on the surface to determine precisely where tunnels lie or whether they have been dug on the right claims. Sometimes heavy vehicle operators, believing they are driving safely between claims, precipitate cave-ins.

Virginia Grant

Digging without a plan or posted tunnel locations can be dangerous for the miner working underground. When others drive on top of active claims, they can cause cave-ins. Fortunately, this collapse (left) occurred at night, when the shaft was unoccupied.

Lightning Ridge has limited water. The need for cooperative plants to wash gravel (far right) is obvious, even to its motley collection of independent-minded miners. When wet, opal colors are easier to spot.

Black opal nobbies, distinctive Lightning Ridge shapes, typically form with potch on one side or between potch layers (right). Before the stones are cut, value can only be estimated. Miners usually have their finds cut immediately, so they can collect the added value from offering finished pieces to waiting buyers.

Lightning Ridge stands apart from other opal fields. Its opal, with dark backgrounds, has no counterpart other than stones at Mintabie, which produces approximately twenty percent black opal. Unlike the country's remote desert center, with a blistering, almost unlivable climate, the cooler location of the Ridge, with enough moisture to support scrub trees and proximity to east coast cities, encourages stable growth.

The Ridge has water most of the year sufficient for groups of miners to form wash cooperatives. It is far easier to separate opal visually in wet gravel. Once out of the mine, opal dirt goes by tip-truck to one of several dam sites, where it is dumped into an agitator with water spraying in from the top. As the dirt tumbles for four to five hours, sludge oozes from the agitator sides, leaving wet pebbles and rocks the size of peas to watermelons. These are "tailed out" down a sloping tray, where the miners inspect each piece by hand. Anything promising they toss into a bucket. Anything really promising they lick or dip into water first to make sure it has color. All the while, the gooey silt washes to the bottom of the dam site, creating a surreal milky gray pond. Solid debris, the rocks and pebbles, form "mullock heaps" near the top of the dam site. The miners happily carry their new opal finds back to the mine for further cleaning and examination to determine which stones to cut.

Many changes have occurred since Char-lie Nettleton walked in from the bush in 1902, when there were no more than seven men digging for opal on the Ridge. Now a local character named Spider, who mines a bit and sells to the Chinaman at the motel on Opal Street, complains, "I've been

Karen Lindley Pty. Ltd.

Karen Lindley Pty. Ltd.

here since I was three. Just at this place. There's more than 15,000 people here now. Crowded. We wish they'd all go home and leave us alone." His census is probably not far off. Another miner, who, typically, insists on anonymity, noted, "Only 1800 people declare themselves Lightning Ridge residents, so they can vote, but 7500 pick up their mail at the post office. I'd say about a 100 miners make a whole lot of money, and about 50 are plain filthy rich."

The most amazing change from the old days is that there is a town at all. Many mining communities still have nothing but dirt streets and shanties, brothels, and a few bars. The Ridge, however, looks downright citified, with pavement, a bowling club, parks, private-club gambling, comfortable motels, restaurants, well-stocked groceries, and liquor stores. A sometimes rowdy, always packed pub sports a suitably understated sign over the bar, "If assholes could fly—this place would be an international airport."

Many developing countries only mine gems, letting foreign cutting centers earn the extra value by selling finished stones. In fact, most gems of all types are cut in countries other than where they were mined. Diamonds found in Africa, Australia, and Russia typically are cut and polished in Israel, India, and Belgium. Rubies and sapphires mined globally are cut in Thailand. Even though Australia is not Third World, for decades it has sent most of its sapphire to Thailand uncut, and it still ships the majority of Coober Pedy and Mintabie opal as rough to Hong Kong and mainland China. Only Lightning Ridge operates as both—a major opal mining area and a cutting center.

George Brooks & Schorr Marketing

Miners, who are usually not cutters, want to maximize profits from their pricy gems, so they support a cutting business unlike any other in Australia. Ridge cutters specialize in black opal, producing uncalibrated hand-held native cuts from local nobbies and rough.

Stones almost always leave the Ridge cut, polished, and ready to mount. High quality black opal pieces are usually cabbed as ovals, thick and robust, with or without potch backings. When a miner with new opal has cash, he hires a cutter, and they agree on the rough's worth based on the fixed price of A$5 to cut a piece of rough worth A$250. When the miner is broke, which is usual, he partners with the cutter, giving up two-and-a-half percent of the selling price for the service.

Every mine, every shack, every restaurant, every crossroads serves as a wholesale venue, particularly the motel and its parking lot at the main intersection. The whole town cheerfully engages in the mission of moving black opal from Lightning Ridge around the globe. Buyers come to town continually, either to deal with specific miners they know in advance have opal or to take their chances by setting up shop at the motel. Once there, they write their name and room number on an outside chalk board and open their doors for business. Anyone with rough or finished opal shows goods, gets an instant offer, and collects cash on the spot. As few opals are consumed domestically, most of the buyers represent companies that sell overseas.

Great stones usually go to Japan, some to Hong Kong, Singapore, and Bangkok, and rarely a few to the USA. I asked Dag Johnson, a Norwegian adventurer-dealer who started mining Australian opal in 1955, where the good black opal sells. Thinking for a minute, he estimated that out of a 100, about 90 go to Japan, 2 to the USA, and the rest elsewhere in Asia. China is now a major cutting center for light opal, but it consumes only the lower qualities. Other Asian countries buy the extremes, the low to medium qualities as well as the world's most expensive black, boulder, and light opal.

E. Gregory Sherman, Pty. Ltd.

When miners either don't have the funds to hire cutters or they find material better sold uncut, they tour Lightning Ridge's known haunts for waiting buyers. "Spider," left, offers uncut rough to a Chinese buyer who will have it cut in either Hong Kong or China. Locally-cut opals are almost always free-hand ovals, shaped to maximize weight retention.

I talked with Karen Lindley, a well-known Sydney black opal dealer, and with exporters of Australia's light and boulder opal about Asian collecting enthusiasm. All had ideas about why Asians instead of Americans buy the best. Considering that large great opals have been available from Australia only this century, there is no grand tradition, but there is a sense that opal is a gem with special qualities. In America the high cost of fine individual stones and concern about spending so much on a gem that may craze or crack are probably factors. Karen points out that she seldom hears such apprehension in Korea, where opal symbolizes eternal love and happiness, or in Japan, where it connotes good fortune. She says opal is "bad luck" only if you don't own one. As a result of USA buyer resistance, she takes her best black opal directly to Tokyo and Bangkok, where customers add opals of various hues and patterns to their growing gem collections. They adore opal's colors and appreciate the gem's uniqueness. Consequently, few Americans ever see Australia's best.

Buying for the high end of the market is different from most of the commerce proceeding around the Ridge's main intersection. Sometimes great opal, like the gorgeous harlequin specimen on the cover, does pass through the motel's parking lot. However, big buyers of fine opal often prefer operating from their motel rooms or visiting miners at their claims or some other secluded location. Usually, having known each other for years, the miners and buyers have long ago worked out terms and the type, size, and quality opal desired. Time being valuable and travel expensive, regular buyers call in advance to register their wish lists and to assure new stones are available. Opal mining differs from manufacturing, where managers can plan ahead, buy raw materials,

As if waiting for Cyrano de Bergerac to intone, "I must go up to the opaline moon...," here shines a heavenly opal orb worthy of the poet's beloved Roxanne.

Virginia Grant

17

Horse trading and opal selling have everything in common. The process of gems changing hands reaches high art at Lightning Ridge. First comes a priceless hour playing cat and mouse. One of the masters, "Ivan," lounged in his trailer (left) before an oil-cloth table piled high with a buyer's cash and nine black opals, which he offered for A$600,000.

and make a known number of like products to sell. Obviously, no one can predict what a miner will find. And no two gems will be alike. Every aspect of the opal business is unpredictable.

For two days recently I accompanied Karen Lindley around Lightning Ridge, as she added black opals to her considerable inventory in preparation for an upcoming show in Tokyo. A week before our chartered flight, Karen started calling to find out who had what. She left messages, asked questions, made appointments, and gathered cash. Beginning to look at opals immediately after breakfast, she met each seller with his or her small plastic bags of polished goods or containers of uncut opal. While her partner examined gems in the motel's courtyard, where he could position himself with a northern exposure for even light, Karen met inside with cutters and miners. She eyed each stone briefly, first by diffused daylight from the window, then with a small flashlight. She explained, "I don't want opal that looks good only in daylight or only at night. At this price point, a fine black opal must exhibit great play-of-color. And it has to have been cut right to show off that color."

We next moved around Lightning Ridge, which is quite small, dropping in on cutters and miners to shop for new material. She spoke to cutters already working on opal she had bought as rough and picked up pieces finished for her Tokyo trip. The cutters showed some stones they owned alone and some they held jointly with other miners. After viewing each gem by daylight and flashlight, she ac-

Ivan's Collection

Karen Lindley Pty. Ltd.

The classic game is one of wit and patience, dodging and bluffing. Ivan owns the gems. Karen Lindley, Sydney dealer, wants to purchase some to show in Tokyo within a few days. Old friends, they drink beer, joke, offer and counter-offer. She ends the transaction by buying two of his nine black opals.

cepted a few, which went into her Tokyo bag. Money changed hands, and by then word had spread around town, so other miners with goods came looking for Karen.

Soon we drove to a claim that everyone in our party agreed would have more great black opal than anywhere else on the Ridge. Remembering the general disdain local residents have for last names, I was not surprised they introduced the owner as "Ivan," nothing more. It turns out that Ivan (now deceased) was a famous fixture at Lightning Ridge. Many new miners waited to see where he would settle before staking their claims. Having mined for longer than most people can remember, Ivan had shown an uncanny ability over the decades for choosing the right place to uncover outstanding opal.

Today was proof of his prowess. Lounging before an oil-cloth-covered card table inside the dilapidated immobile trailer he called home, Ivan rolled out nine large impressive blue-green opals. Eyeing Karen's reaction sideways while offering her a beer, he watched her roll each gem around in her fingers before revealing his price, A$600,000 for the lot. She did not want them all, she told him, as she piled A$50 and A$100 bills on the small table. The negotiation had begun. In less than half an hour, Karen had two new black opals, Ivan had the stack of cash, and I had my photographs. A pair of Japanese would soon be proud owners of two fine new gems. Just another day on the Ridge, a Mecca for eccentrics and home of the finest, most expensive, and generally most desirable opal in the world.

Two recent events illustrate how much pride Australians take in their opal. In 1993 the government officially proclaimed opal the National Gemstone of Australia. Then, in 1995 two holographic postage stamps acknowledged the honor; this one for black opal, and one for light opal on page 45.

19

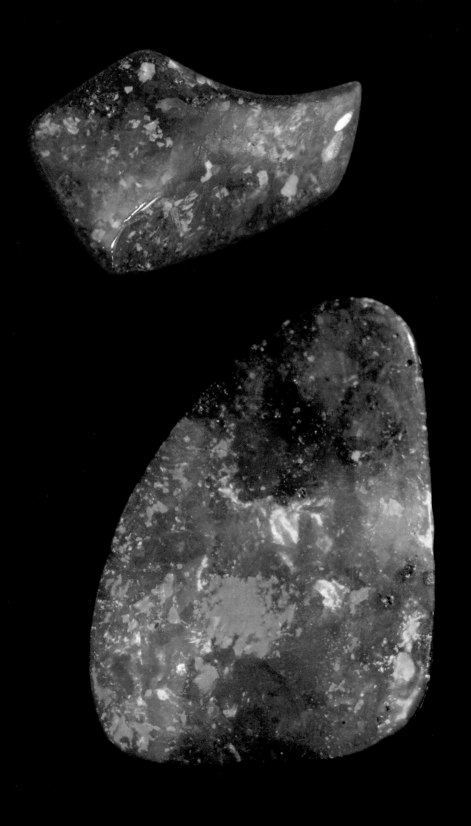

BOULDER

OPAL

L ike some prehistoric foraging beast, the giant orange arm swung broadly over the reddish brown landscape. Three of us scrambled below the excavator, alternately dodging the swinging bucket and dashing under it to check the fruits of its work. As each scrape removed a few more inches of sandstone, we drew that much closer to dark seams that might hold boulder opal. When only an inch or so of host dirt remained above what might be gem seams, we wielded small picks to carefully extract likely chunks of ironstone. Flashes of color around the edges suggested hidden riches that had lain underground for millions of years. Popped open, most contained nothing of value. Several came agonizingly close, with traces of opal to whet our appetite but not enough thickness for gemstones. A precious few gleamed with intense colors, explosions of purples, reds, and greens.

Treasure hunting in opal mines is "up close and personal." No international conglomerates clutter the landscape with pin-striped suits and briefcases. No big mining firms fill the hills with office buildings. No syndicate ties up output. One-on-one digging yields total independence for a lone miner with a dream. A middle-aged claim holder sidled up to me one morning, saying, "I've mined all my life. I don't know any other business where you can wake up dead broke, make a strike, be a millionaire by noon, and have that million dollars in your pocket in cash by dinner."

When miners hit precious opal, they immediately see both color and play-of-color. Their instant verification and gratification differs vastly from the feedback workers get in mining most other gems and the jewelry metals. Generally, gold, silver, and platinum miners never see the metal, which they move as ore to a processor in a distant closed building. Almost no diamond miners (except along Africa's west coast) ever see a gem. Again, they move

Precious Opal ———→  ←——— Ironstone

Boulder opal, from Queensland in eastern Australia, owes much of its popularity to designers who love working with brilliant colors and freeform shapes. Cracks in ironstone provided space for the dramatic opal's formation. Boulder opals are cut to retain an ironstone backing.

Left top: Central Australian Opal Mines; Bottom: Berta Opal Company, Pty. Ltd.

Near Quilpie, in Queensland, miners Sandy Kent and Ken Phillips use an excavator (left) to expose opal seams (above). Then they wield picks to remove chunks of ironstone containing opal. Sandy exults, "It's like holding a moonbeam in my hands."

tons of dirt to a plant that separates diamonds from kimberlite and gravel by a sophisticated robotic process. The splendid color of rubies and sapphires remains veiled until cleaning, heat-treating, cutting, and polishing slowly turn unimpressive rough into gorgeous jewels. And it takes cutting, polishing, and enhancements to transform rough emerald crystals into saleable gems.

The appearance of opal improves with cutting and polishing of course. But no matter if miners are picking away in a dark underground tunnel or working the level on the shear side of an open cut, once they see color, there is no tantalizing wait for satisfaction. How lucky the opal miner, who knows every day whether he has found treasure. And usually, when he does hit opal, he knows that treasure belongs to him alone.

Quilpie is normally a hard three-day dirt road drive from Sydney. Instead of traveling by car, for research on this book I accompanied opal dealers who had chartered a small plane for a buying trip. Our "airport" consisted of a private dirt strip in the middle of a large sheep station (farm) fifty miles from nowhere. After Sandy Kent, the miner we had come to see, had shooed the cows off the runway, we cleared the low scrub growth to land amid moos of protest and barks of welcome from a pack of herd dogs. Rattling away in his truck over five miles of trackless hard scrabble, we arrived at Sandy's fifty-acre lease.

In an isolated camp spread over a low sandstone hill, with a generator, refrigerator, fresh water tanked from the farm, and a trailer, Sandy and his partner had made the primitive comfortable. Before their three-sided outhouse, affording a panoramic view of the bush, passed Australian fauna, from flocks of gray-and-salmon-colored *galahs* to a neighborly kangaroo. Because she and her offspring had become the camp mascots, they had been spared. But the station owners need meat for themselves and their dogs, so they hunt 'roos by motorbike throughout their property.

Budgerigars, parrots as bright as Sandy's boulder opal, flashed and rustled in the wattles, acacia trees, beside the patio. Even with an often reckless wind and near-freezing nights, the camp was more like a wilderness vacation spot than a mine. Marveling at the foamy Milky Way overhead, one might have thought Sandy had picked the site for stargazing. Rather, he had carefully scanned aerial photographs that suggested alignment of joints where silica-laden water might have entered the ground to form opal. As we walked his claim, Sandy showed me the additional good indicators of widely scattered weathered opal pieces and test holes probably from the 1800s.

Fortunately for Queensland, it has two opal types, sandstone and boulder. Sandstone opal, which looks like specimens mined at Mintabie or Andamooka, formed unattached, as free opal; boulder opal formed attached to reddish-brown ironstone. By definition and consent of the various Australian gem trade associations, *boulder opal* is "presented in one piece, where the opal is naturally attached to the host rock in which it was formed and the host rock is of a different chemical composition." Boulder opal filled cracks in heavily brecciated ironstone, stone composed of sharp-

Sandy Kent located his mine by studying aerial photographs and finding surface opal deposits apparently worked in the late 1800s. Although not gems, the remnants suggest the richness of the deposit. Sandy finds saleable opals 5-20 feet underground.

The Australian Museum

Because the opal in boulder opal lies as a seam within ironstone, some pieces can be cut or broken directly through the color seam to produce unique boulder opal "splits" (see right and below). These mirror images make perfect earring gems. Designers use the repetitive color and pattern to create one-of-a-kind jewelry.

angled fragments embedded in a fine-grained matrix. Opal seams, as well as thin strips or bands of opal, course through the rock, indicating where silica-laden water once seeped into all available spaces.

Sensing no one would buy opal with a brown stone backing, early miners set about to cut or break the opal away from the ironstone. If successful, they sold the gems as *Queensland opal*; if not, they discarded the shards. Initially countless millions of dollars of unwanted scraps were left in the fields. Sometimes, dubbing pretty bits of thin boulder opal "fun stones," the miners gave them as favors to the women in camp. Unlike any other opal mined, boulder opal took years to be appreciated. Until the 1970s, there was almost no market for it. As the most vivid and the most stable of opal types, today boulder opal rivals black opal in price.

Both sandstone and boulder opal seem to have been first mined in Queensland in 1872. Only sandstone opal and boulder opal cut free of its ironstone were offered for sale. Their successful appearance at an 1873 London gem exhibition must have sparked further exploration because a number of leases, mines, and sales were documented between 1873 and 1888. One opal sold in London for A£150, the equivalent of about three years' wages. Tales of such riches whetted appetites.

Just as he would later play a pivotal role in the marketing of black opal, Tully Wollaston almost single-handedly introduced Queensland sandstone opal to the world. It was late in 1888 when he received a visitor in Adelaide, on Australia's southern coast. The visitor told of wonderful new opal he had seen three years before in Queensland. Solely on his guest's description, with no assurance that the miner was still alive, Wollaston and his guest and an Aboriginal boy embarked on a dangerous desert sojourn.

Setting out on camels across southern Australia, they braved blistering summer heat, the worst weather ever seen in that area of the young country. Seven brutal weeks and 1100 kilometers later, the trio found their miner, Joe Bridle, who introduced them to other opal "gougers."

Weeks of darting and feinting, thrusting and parrying dragged on until they had established sufficient trust for deal-making. Wollaston

Robert Shapiro

24

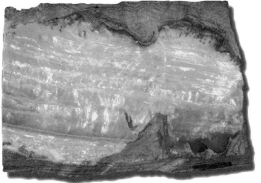

Opal from Little Wonder Mine, Queensland, courtesy Opal Country, Itzehoe, Germany

bought Joe's first parcel of sixty-one opals for A£27, half a year's wages. With the mainly sandstone opal parcel, Wollaston made his way to Brisbane and by boat back to Adelaide, staying only a few days before sailing for London. Once there, he faced seemingly endless rejection from gem dealers happy to buy less colorful Hungarian material instead of his. Finally, one firm in London's Hatton Gardens jewelry district recognized the potential of an opal brighter and more beautiful than any Hungarian material. The company hired cutters and marketed the new opal both in England and in America. What Wollaston began burgeoned into an international industry.

Herbert Bond first tried to market boulder opal as such in 1875, even selling public shares in London in 1879. He failed, but others successfully sold the material thick enough to yield gems with its ironstone removed. Interest in Queensland opal grew until new, larger, and more lucrative opal fields lured miners away. At the turn of the century White Cliffs operated just across the border in New South Wales. Lightning Ridge began commercial production in 1903, followed by the huge discoveries in South Australia at Coober Pedy, Mintabie, and Andamooka. Those gains resulted in corollary losses for Queensland. Boulder opal activity, never strong, was limited to only one mine in 1955 and no more than six in 1961.

The introduction of heavy earth-moving equipment and diamond saws, which easily cut ironstone, revolutionized boulder opal mining during the 1960s. Global opal awareness in the 1970s brought even more mining activity, reviving sales that peaked at A$6.6 million in 1988, then, due to new government regulations, declined to less than A$2 million. Because of its brilliant colors and durability, as well as aggressive marketing, boulder opal sales are climbing again.

Boulder opal fields extend throughout most of southern Queensland, from Hungerford to Winton. Much of the mining activity centers around Quilpie, in the south, and Opalton, near the center of Queensland. Even with recent opal promotions and increasing public awareness, generally fewer than a hundred operators at a time mine claims, 100 x 100 meters at Yowah and Opalton, unlimited in size elsewhere. As at other opal fields, some boulder opal miners work for themselves, some with

Evert Opals

25

partners, and some for small mining companies. As more miners bring in huge earth-moving equipment to facilitate serious surface mining, fewer work underground blasting and clearing tunnels.

Intense colors usually attract buyers, and for color intensity, boulder opal is without peer. Look at the brilliance and color purity of samples at the bottom of page 24 and to the left. No other opal type can match the impact of large vibrant color spots that appear to roll across the gems with every turn. A similar dark background that makes black opal special also contributes to the drama of boulder opal. Opaque ironstone works the same as black body tone or black potch to accent and emphasize play-of-color.

Robert Shapiro

Among its many charms, boulder's three-dimensionality allows designers to emphasize surface contours in custom-designed jewelry. Another unique feature makes boulder opal exceedingly popular especially for matched earrings. Because the opal forms surrounded by ironstone, often a newly-mined piece can be opened by splitting the host directly through the opal seam to reveal mirror-image gems. "Splits" with great color and pattern are as rare as matched emeralds, rubies, or colored diamonds, and priced accordingly, sometimes wholesaling for $5,000 to $30,000 a pair. Matched gem pairs are worth more than twice the cost of a similar-quality single jewel.

Include durability as an often overlooked benefit of boulder opal. With large ironstone backings, boulders are tough. In addition, water content within the opal is low, usually only a few percent. As a result, boulder opal almost never cracks or crazes as it ages. In direct contrast, sometimes more than half the newly mined opal from various volcanic sources around the world craze within minutes of exposure to air (see page 40). Boulder opal stability gives it a substantial advantage in the market.

Nevertheless, marketing boulder opal remains a paradox. Because so much of its weight is ironstone, it is the only opal type usually sold by the piece rather than by the carat. You can see from the photographs that boulder's colors are typically more dramatic than other opal types, a quality experienced buyers appreciate. But most potential customers do not even recognize the name *boulder opal* nor understand its benefits and distinctiveness. When I extol its virtues, most people ask if they are rocks painted with opal, or doublets, or something altogether new.

Once explained and shown, boulder opal almost sells itself. Most potential opal buyers, particularly in America, expect opal to be small, solid white, and speckled with tiny dots of color, called *pinfire*; calibrated sizes of them dominate the USA market. Many people have never seen opal both

Endlessly surprising, boulder opal displays different colors and patterns in every piece. This trio, with brilliant reds and distinctive stripes, came from Doreen's "Wonder Mine." Generally boulder opal prices are based on color, opal thickness, size, and overall beauty.

large and beautiful. Customers who compare boulder to black often realize the dramatic look they can get with boulder. A couple of friends I rendez-voused with had waited to come to Australia to shop for an engagement ring. The young woman knew she wanted an opal. First she considered light opal, then black. But once she saw boulder opal, she lost her heart for a second time.

Neither flat, nor faceted, nor domed like its black and light counter-parts, boulder opal undulates across the ironstone face as water flowed there millennia ago. Endowed with beauty and durability, it deserves attention. Certainly some black opal and light opal is deliberately cut to include natural potch backing. In such cases both gem and backing are opal. Not so with boulder opal. Gems usually consist of a thin top of multicolored opal layered onto a thick durable base of ironstone, which is clearly visible from the sides and bottom and occasionally from the top. If host rock shows through the face of the opal, the price goes down.

An obvious question arises here and in several other places in this book. If you have precious opal atop either common opal or another substance, is it a doublet? Not if they formed naturally together. This definition holds for all opal types: If natural precious opal has been cut to include common opal or potch in one piece, the gemstone is a natural opal. If opal has been cut to include ironstone (instead of common opal or potch), the gemstone is a boulder opal. But if someone assembles a piece of natural opal with common opal, potch, or any other material (glass, plastic, onyx, ironstone, etc.), the result is a doublet.

Today's boulder opal often has a huge color range (opposite, bottom) and spectacular patterns (opposite, top) but relatively thin layers of opal. Early in this century when boulder opal was new in the market, choice thick seams were still available. Carved before 1920 from a generous seam, this five-inch long luminous lizard is three-dimensional. Its tail realistically wraps to the underside.

27

Because boulder opal has two parts, the temptation seems great to sell assembled boulder opal doublets for naturals. I recently saw them marketed throughout Australia and found them especially prevalent in Hawaiian shops. It is unfair to misrepresent any material as natural, at the price of natural or less, that has been grown in a laboratory or assembled by people instead of nature. A quick visual exam usually differentiates naturals from doublets. In naturals, a wavy line follows the interface between opal and ironstone, whereas boulder opal doublets usually display a straight junction (see page 21). Use magnification to detect glue in a doublet.

Yowah nuts, a rare and remarkable opal type, remain practically unheard of by the public. Unique to Queensland's boulder opal territory around the tiny community with the same name, a Yowah surprisingly resembles a large ironstone nut. In their once-hollow interiors, some few contain a brilliant opal core. Like quartz geodes, they reveal their interior secrets only when you cut or break apart their hard exteriors (left). With a small single source yielding only a few specimens of attractive opal, Yowahs are usually marketed at gem shows and auctions as collectible display items. Scarcity renders them expensive.

Like boulder opal splits, Yowahs can be separated into mirror images. To keep their name, they must maintain a recognizable part of their nutlike "shell." If cutters preserve only part of the ironstone matrix when extracting the opal, the product is *boulder opal*. If, however, they

Stabler Sapphires & Opal International

Good color and an attractive pattern transform boulder opal matrix into jewelry (left). When the opal distributed throughout ironstone is too small, pale, or scattered for gems, then the matrix itself can become a decorative product. Large pieces are ideal for bookends (opposite) and mosaic tables. Carved animals in boulder opal matrix make particularly popular Australian souvenirs.

Robert Shapiro

completely separate the opal from its ironstone matrix, it would be classified as neither *Yowah* or *boulder*, but *solid opal*.

Boulder matrix opal, ironstone interspersed with precious opal, includes the host rock as a design feature. When boulder opal formed, silica-rich water infiltrated ironstone, filling cracks, crevices, and voids. The larger filled areas produce marketable gem opal. Now Australian and Asian cutters and sculptors fashion entire pieces of matrix with color into hundreds of different products. Their dilemma is how to cut the matrix to retain enough colorful opal to give it visual appeal yet not so much that it looks like jewelry, which prices it out of the carving-material market. Workers cut individual small pieces for inexpensive jewelry cabs and beads, mosaic tables, and bookends; and huge sparkling matrix blocks for decorative wall material, over which water cascades in several upscale Australian stores and office buildings.

Sydney dealer Zoltan Berta, working with a talented team of carvers, features both boulder opal jewelry and sculpted boulder matrix. His work-shop turns out a variety of matrix animals, including eagles, whales, pigs, and the famous "Crocodile Dundee" crocs like the one below, which seems to watch through inscrutable opal eyes for the chance to bite the unwary with its sharp light opal teeth. Zoltan likes making use of an Australian natural resource that miners once tossed aside in opal fields as waste. He talks like a lover about the opal and ironstone combination unique to Queensland, "Wait till you see *my* opal, you will never see more beautiful opal," he kept telling me over the engine drone all the way to Quilpie. "The intensity, the way the colors play, the sharp patterns—like the landscape, like the sunset. Boulder opal eclipses all the others."

Australian crocodiles are famous, thanks to the movies. With a body of boulder opal matrix and opal teeth and eyes, this one bears an disquieting resemblance to the creatures that rule the northern coast.

Berta Opal Company, Pty. Ltd.

29

LIGHT OPAL, CRYSTALS, & FOSSILS

Brilliant sunlight contrasted with the inky-black hole I hesitated to step into. "It's easy," the Coober Pedy miner urged. "Just straddle this board, I'll take care of the rest. This wench has only given way once," he reassured me. "The rest" included walking out into space over a shoulder-width cavity that plunged forty feet straight down into an opal mine. Only once before had I allowed myself to be dropped into a mine by a single line to the surface. Banging against rocky walls on the rapid descent, I thought this time as I had thought then, "What's wrong with ladders anyway?"

But Coober Pedy opal miners think nothing of going to work every day by grabbing a rope and dropping into a hole where they will spend most of their lives. Strangely, the lifestyle they have chosen fits the outback very well, even with the challenges of heat and water. Although the story has been repeated so many times that people now believe it, the words *Coober Pedy* are not Aboriginal for "white man in a hole." They really mean "water hole."

People, though, do live and work underground at Coober Pedy. Obviously the reason they work below is that down under is where the opal is. Many of them also live underground, having scooped rooms horizontally out of hills. In their dugouts, residents in the isolated community avoid the beastly heat that soars to a dangerously high 120° to 140°F during Australian summers, December through February. Even in September, when I stepped into the void that ended in a honeycomb of tunnels, I felt the blessed relief of escaping from the searing cloudless desert day above to a cool, slightly moist Sesame below. And at the end of the day, I hated to leave.

Solid Precious Opal ——→ Precious Opal ←—— Potch ←——

Some beautiful opals look like optical illusions. The stunning pattern in this 9.13-carat translucent Lightning Ridge crystal (opposite) appears to be a rolling liquid. Both examples above are defined as solid opal.

"Dragon's Tear;" Lapidary International

Still isolated, Coober Pedy is a wonderland for gem lovers. Near the center of Australia's desert interior, the storied community remains the world's largest opal producer. Tailings from a century of mining create a bizarre landscape, used as the otherworldly location for Mad Max, *the movie (opposite, below). Miners escape the heat in tunnels formed by digging machines that have slowly eaten away at the opal-bearing level. A vacuum tube sucks up the mined opal dirt (right). Solids fall into a steel drum (left), while dust vents into the air. When the drum is full, gravity tips the contents onto a tailings pile.*

As opal miners in South Australia's "Precious Stone Fields" are exempt from restoration, thousands of unmarked, uncovered shafts surround Coober Pedy, creating a deadly hazard for the unwary.

Coober Pedy, the world's largest light (or white) opal field, looks far different from the gravel and sandstone walls of a black opal tunnel in Lightning Ridge or the stark sandstone cuts at a boulder opal mine near Quilpie. The predominant underground color is cream marbled with dramatic dark pinkish red swirls, a combination so eerily beautiful that motel rooms not dug into the hillsides are painted and shaped like tunnel walls. Called *shale* or *sandstone* by the locals, the earth looks and feels like clay—slick, slightly moist, and sticky. As small mechanical diggers gouge their paths, they imprint entire walls with spirals that resemble pre-Columbian carvings.

Reaching the central Australian town is a pleasant day trip on paved roads or a short flight in a small airplane north from Adelaide or south from Alice Springs. But travel was dramatically different as recently as the 1950s, when Aboriginals outnumbered the few miners twenty to one. Dag Johnson, who came from Norway to see the Olympics and stayed to dig opal, recounts a harrowing trek.

"The mail truck went from Kingoonya to Coober Pedy every Friday," Dag recalls. "It was vital to leave a day or two before, so if you really broke down, the mail driver would find you along the way. Otherwise, you probably

Jayson Traurig Bros. of Australia

would never have walked out. Remember, there were no roads in the '50s. You just followed ruts into the desert. And you had to take everything—food, water, petrol, spares, anything you would need to travel or mine. Bumping in the ruts damaged the differential. You'd keep adding all the oil you had, then stuff it with bananas. We measured trips by blowouts, not miles, like saying it was 'a four-tire trip.' After a while we'd run out of spare tires, tubes, and patches, so we'd wrap the tires with bailing wire and fill 'em with our clothes. Many a night I'd arrive in Coober Pedy dressed only in my undershorts."

Now Coober Pedy boasts more than a thousand residents, civic clubs, a three-and-a-half star hotel, and buildings above ground. Tourism brings in a lot of money, but not as much as opal. Mining itself has changed, having become a little more scientific, though it still attracts free-spirited loners. The area produces most of Australia's light opal, which generally falls into three categories: Large important pieces that sell singly; small calibrated solid opal cabs for affordable jewelry; and opal too pale, too thin, or too fragile to use in anything but inexpensive jewelry or the lowest-priced triplets.

Most opal sold in the USA is white (or light). Coober Pedy's specialty, light opal, is but one type. By volume more light opal is mined than black or boulder opal. The best light (left except for the two black opals at 7 o'clock and 8 o'clock, and below right) rarely reaches American markets, going instead to Asia.

To escape Coober Pedy's blistering summer heat, miners often live in dugouts, homes carved into the hillsides. Few offer such luxury as this indoor pool (below).

Umoona Opal Mine & Museum

American dealer George Manning is largely credited with having transformed Coober Pedy in the 1960s. He promoted small standardized sizes suited to jewelry manufacture. Manning bought huge quantities of opal rough, which created a mining boom, and shipped it to Hong Kong for cutting. Then he sold the oval opal cabs in the USA. Manning's and others' initiatives account for much of Americans' continued purchase of light opal, the N7, N8, and N9 body tones in the new Australian opal nomenclature.

As in other opal mining areas, Coober Pedy miners run all-cash, no-records, no-receipts enterprises. In 1966 the South Australia government proposed a bill requiring receipts and taxes on opal transactions. Opal miners dug in their picks. Showing superior organizational skills, they joined with buyers, threatening legislators that if they were taxed like mere mortals, they would bring the opal trade to a halt. The government agreed to back off, tax subsequent opal sales instead, and not raise the issue again.

Mintabie is regarded as an unusual opal field because it produces good quantities and qualities of all three opal body tones—black, dark, and light opal, sometimes in a single opal pocket. Off Stuart Highway, I gingerly navigated twenty-two bumpy miles into an Aboriginal reservation to "town center," the dusty locus of five dirt roads and a general store. For any misgivings, I found the community downright charming. The first thing I noticed was a shiny new sign posted in front of the government's mine office begging miners coming for claim stakes and licenses to open the gate—instead of plowing straight through the fence. When I stopped to call my contact, I met an untethered pet camel loitering about the pub angling for a handout. You have to love a town with character like this.

Faye's underground house, Coober Pedy

S. David Brookes

Three hours north of Coober Pedy, Mintabie remains almost unknown outside the opal trade, although twice it outproduced its famous neighbor. Even the airport has to go because opals lie beneath it (above). Mintabie produces a variety of opal in all three body tones, black, dark, and light, sometimes as large as this huge 28-ounce blue-green specimen (left) from nearby Lambina and the colorful opal and sandstone example below.

Imagine my delight to meet a gentleman opal miner in the *never-never*, which is how Aboriginals refer to the outback. Educated and erudite, a savvy cutter and retailer as well, Peter Blythe stays in touch with the market through an attractive shop in Canberra. With partner Peter Noakes, he digs half the year at Mintabie. His compatriots classify him as a "good miner," a high compliment indeed. For his fellow miners he performs a free service of valuing their new finds so they will know what to charge Aussie and Chinese buyers on weekend rounds from Coober Pedy.

The two Peters work underground. I scuttled down a narrow fifty-foot ladder bolted to the side of a three-foot shaft to where Peter B. was setting the last of eight charges to blast out the side of a tunnel. After tamping sandstone around the fertilizer and diesel mixture, he grabbed a sparkler off the wall to light the circular pigtails of fuses. I yelled, "How long do we have?" "Oh, plenty," he said. "By the time these blow, we'll be up top, resting on the bumper, having a cup of tea." I scrambled back up that ladder fast, and I could hear him just behind me counting. Sure enough, at 110 seconds, when eight blasts two

Umoona Opal Mine
& Museum

E. Gregory
Sherman, Pty. Ltd.

Berta Opal Co. Pty. Ltd.

seconds apart shook the ground, we were leaning against the truck chatting.

Although tunneling remains the pattern at Coober Pedy and was the norm in the heyday at Andamooka, most other miners at Mintabie open-cut. To compare, Lightning Ridge mines almost all black opal underground, and Queensland mainly uses surface mining for boulder opal. Open-cuts pay in three specific circumstances: When opal seams lie close to the surface; when opal occurs in relatively close-together shallow seams; or when opal occurs throughout the host material rather than in level seams.

Mintabie's random distribution makes digging out an entire claim necessary, even as deep as 100 feet. Every untouched inch may contain precious opal. At Coober Pedy, opal occurs in fairly regular horizontal seams. Miners need only tunnel at seam levels, ignoring most of the underground claim between. Other considerations as well moved Mintabie toward strip mining. Tunneling machines that work efficiently with Coober Pedy's soft

In addition to opals, Mintabie has character, with a wooly frontier feel that appeals to its resident free-spirits and a devil-may-care attitude that fits its anonymous population. As signs of the times, one message pleads to watch out for planes before blasting, while another, at the government mining office, pleads with miners to open the gate instead of crashing through for claim stakes and licenses.

Peter Blythe has blasted out a tunnel (far left) about 50 feet below ground. He divides his time between mining and operating a retail store in Canberra. His partner, Peter Noakes (left), determines where to dig by dousing with divining rods to find faults, or slips, which miners believe lead to opal deposits below. A friend of the Peters often foretold opal finds in his dreams.

moist clay would slow to a crawl in Mintabie's hard coarse sandstone; and blowers that easily lift Coober Pedy's opal dirt to the surface, would quickly wear out transporting Mintabie's abrasive host rock.

Miners of most other ore consider opal plots—only 50 x 50 or 50 x 100 meters—too small for strip mining; gem values makes them financially viable. A Croatian miner changed Mintabie attitudes when he made a great deal of money by staking three adjacent claims and buying enough earth-moving equipment to shift every particle of dirt from one claim to another after he had checked it for opal. Consequently, having rooted through the sandstone fields with bulldozers for years, miners have transfigured the landscape around Mintabie into a moonscape. And as South Australia excludes "Precious Stone Fields" from restoration requirements, miners can walk away with the opal, leaving claims the way they dug them.

Another instance of Mintabie adaptability involves the airport. Even though miners originally sited it precisely where they had considered the land unpromising, they have since discovered a wealth of opal by the airstrip. Expeditiously, they held a drawing for claims, creating what they laughingly call "millionaires' row." Having constricted the runway to the bare minimum, on the next ballot they vote whether to dig up the airstrip entirely.

Andamooka, a rugged, ragged little town, lies about 150 miles southeast of Coober Pedy. Most of the years between the early 1930s, when it was nothing more than a hot dry spot in the desert, and the 1980s, when its massive opal deposits waned, Andamooka supplied more gem opals than any other area. It probably peaked in the 1960s, when millions of dollars of opal emerged from its barren landscape each year.

Umoona Opal Mine & Museum

Andamooka's fame rests with two opal types, large colorful material, such as the massive 25-kilogram specimen (left), and a unique matrix, which turns black when smoked or sugar-treated (opposite).

The Koninderie (Rainbow) Opal

N otorious as the last best frontier town in the outback, Andamooka built its reputation one bullet at a time. It operated like the Old West from the 1930s, when opal was discovered, until 1966, when it got its first policeman. But even with a legal presence, the authorities had the foresight to rotate officers every few weeks to limit temptation. With valuable opals stashed in coffee cans, tempers could run hot, and guns were as common as boots. Before the town's decline, its best restaurant was the Tucker Box, whose ceiling was plastered with beer bottle labels. The explanation: "To cover the bullet holes."

One wonders how far a mining community should be left to act like a mining community. A kid shot a mate in the school yard while playing cowboys-and-Indians with real guns. Then there was the miner who, near dawn, accidentally plugged his partner, thinking he was a wild dog stealing kangaroo meat. He and his still-conscious partner spent all morning with a pocket knife trying to dig out the slug as it moved from his thigh to his hip. According to local newspapers, at age twenty-five, Dag Johnson was dubbed the "uncrowned king of Andamooka," after having survived the opal fields for only nine years. At that time a reporter quoted Dag saying fourteen people had been shot since he had arrived, but only three had died.

Dag owned the only mansion in town, an air-conditioned novelty with a plastic swimming pool. For months before he personally trucked it across half of Australia, he had collected water to fill it. Then he turned his back yard into a beer garden, not for beauty but for business. He says there was no better way to buy opal than to invite a parched, tired, lonely,

For six decades Andamooka has mined fine light and crystal opal. Occasionally someone still finds gem-quality stones, like the "Andamooka Peacock," but now the area is more often known as the source of treated matrix opal. Located a few hours by car southeast of Coober Pedy, it was worked so heavily that today Coober Pedy and Mintabie far overshadow Andamooka for production.

Central Australian Opal Mines

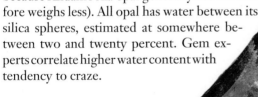

Treating Andamooka matrix to resemble black opal is the most common opal enhancement. Treaters soak light opal in a heated sugar solution, after which they plunge the matrix into sulfuric acid. Released carbon darkens the stone's body tone. To detect Andamooka matrix, expect lighter weight, and look for a black peppery appearance with speckled play-of-color.

Central Australian Opal Mines

broke miner out back prior to negotiating. Needless to say, after a shower, a dip in the pool, and a few cold beers on tap, the miner did not stand a chance.

Andamooka matrix, peculiar to Andamooka, can be treated to darken its body tone. Dag says that when Snyder's store burned about 1960, some opal stored in glycerine-filled jars came out resembling black opal. Scientists at Adelaide University told some of the miners how to duplicate the effect. Two processes capitalize on the porous nature of local matrix as well as some matrix found in other countries. Both produce a dark background that emphasizes any play-of-color in the material.

One treatment begins with heating to drive out water and open the pores. Next the matrix is placed in a heated glucose, lactose, or sugar solution, then dunked into sulfuric acid to release carbon from the sugar into the open pores. The other process involves smoking the opal much as one would smoke a ham, which causes sooty particles to infiltrate the matrix. Some treaters roast matrix in paper; others first soak it in motor oil. The most exotic smoking recipe calls for charcoaling matrix in a brown bag, or clay pot, filled with manure. Few gemologists want to give such treated matrix the tongue test to check for a typically dried-out surface.

Although treated matrix bears the town's name, Andamooka deserves credit for what some call the best opal ever mined. Always in competition with nearby Coober Pedy, Andamooka miners used to brag that their opal was least likely to crack or craze. Their claim appears to have been true, because Andamooka opal generally has the lowest water content (and therefore weighs less). All opal has water between its silica spheres, estimated at somewhere between two and twenty percent. Gem experts correlate higher water content with tendency to craze.

The treater's skill with a 10,500-carat specimen produced this mountain of Andamooka matrix. Usually matrix opals are already cut as gems before they are treated.

Edrin Inc.

The USA mines a variety of fine opal that is mainly known only to collectors. Virgin Valley, Nevada produces spectacular specimens, such as the 61.7-carat carved crystal (near right), discovered in 1993, and contra luz *(against the light) opal (far right). Brilliant flashes of color float within this clear crystal when light enters the gem from the side and back.*

All opal contains water, which begins to evaporate after mining. USA opals are plagued with a tendency to fracture as they lose moisture. An Oregon opal fresh from the ground (left, top) crazes (left, bottom) after only thirty minutes in the air.

West Coast Gemstones, Inc.

Crystal opal displays two distinctive characteristics—play-of-color and transparency. In gemological terms, *crystal opal* does not refer to a crystalline structure but to a crystalline appearance; that is, crystal opal is transparent or semitransparent. Although USA appraisers use the definition, "clear enough to read through," other countries do not follow as strict a guideline. When viewed against a dark or black background, crystal opal can look like a typical colorful gem; when you place it on a light background, you can see through it (below). Technically, any mine can yield opal that creates this illusion. As you might imagine, crystal opal is one of the rarer, more expensive, collectible opal varieties. Andamooka was famous for its crystals, and Coober Pedy still produces some.

A pleasant surprise for American gem buyers may be that several states in the USA mine gem-quality crystal opal, including Nevada, Oregon, and Idaho. Leading the group in uniqueness, rarity, and spectacular color is the almost unknown source at Virgin Valley, Nevada. John S. White, the former Curator of Gems and Minerals at the Smithsonian Institution, said in a burst of admiration, "Were it not for its unfortunate tendency to craze, Virgin Valley opal would surpass all other opal in terms of beauty."

John is absolutely right about crazing. The amazing specimens that

By definition crystal opal *is clear enough to read through. It can occur with any body color. Identically thin butterfly wings were cut from a single piece of opal. When viewed against black, each shimmers with blue, green, and aqua play-of-color; when placed on white, most of its color metamorphoses to a glassy transparency.*

John Anthony Jewelers

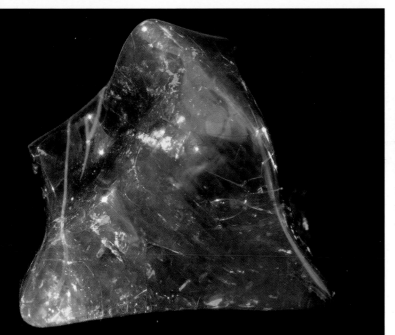

Opal Country, Itzehoe, Germany

come from Virgin Valley almost all craze in time. Even the face of the most famous opal in the Smithsonian's collection, the huge vibrant *Roebling Opal* (right), has visible cracks radiating from its core. The 2665-carat piece, which was found at Virgin Valley's Rainbow Ridge mine in 1919, most likely is replacement opal in the shape of a tree limb or a small log.

Even though the two large Virgin Valley opals on this page are dark, they should not be confused with Australia's black opal, which is translucent to opaque. The transparent nature of crystal opal gives polished gems a shiny vitreous appearance. Compare the softer, almost matte finish on the Andean common opal below with the surface of the Roebling. When I held it, I thought the Roebling Opal looked like glass.

Contra luz material, crystal opal with color play visible only in back or side light, can come from any mine. Some of the best ever found are from Virgin Valley, such as the 36-carat beauty above. Found in 1956 and cut in 1988, it is the removable centerstone in a $30,000 pendant.

Translucent blue opal was used by native South Americans for more than a thousand years. Known as Peruvian *or* Andean opal *and commercially mined near San Patricio, Peru, most of the blue or blue-green material is used for carving. There is some evidence that trace amounts of copper may affect the blue in Andean opals.*

Courtesy Andrew Herman

41

Fossils may be either all opal or part opal. Opal fossils, such as the seashell below, formed in voids as solid opal the size and shape of the original organisms. The partially-opalized snail (left) contains fossil remains of its original shell, along with some opal replacement.

O pal fossils, millions of years old, offer windows to the past and beautiful evidence of how opal forms. From the viewpoint of percentages, it may seem amazing that so many gems have surfaced in organic shapes. But once we understand how most opal originated, it seems logical that we would uncover opal fossils.

As miners find most Australian opal in sedimentary deposits near the ancient seashore of the Great Artesian Basin, we might expect most opal fossils to be of sea creatures. Many scientists agree on the theory that opal formed when silica-saturated water seeped through the ground, filling available spaces and occasionally being stopped by layers of harder material or clay. (A new theory has the water and silica being forced upward; the opal would have been the same.)

Imagine the spaces where silica-rich water might have settled. Sometimes they would have been above impervious rock or clay layers. Openings in rocks would have stopped and held the water. But opals that resulted from such beginnings are not fossils. Next imagine a muddy, silty coastline where shells, bones, wood, and other organic materials sank and decayed. The impressions of their shapes in the solidifying sea bottom are the origin of opal fossils.

Over time the inland sea receded. It left in its wake dry land dotted with small underground voids from dissolved fossils that acted like molds, physical records of life millions of years before. Next came more years of rainfall and surface weathering, which released silica. The silica-laden water

Many materials may be replaced with opal. Found in 1976 in Shellpatch at Coober Pedy, this colorful specimen mirrors a rib from its extinct original, a Mesozoic plesiosaur, a long-necked, small-headed marine reptile.

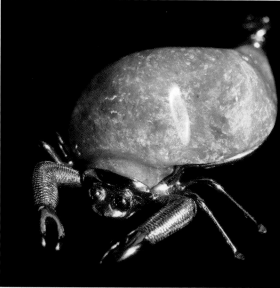

Australia's opal fossils are often from marine creatures. A fossil seashell (right) serves as a crab's body in this new brooch. The internal skeletons of extinct cephalopods, relatives of today's octopi and cuttlefish, may have opalized into what the Aussies call a **pipe***. In the imaginative pin (above), a pipe becomes a shrimp's body.*

E. Gregory Sherman, Pty. Ltd. (both)

seeped through the earth's surface, occupying all available spaces, including voids left by once-living creatures and objects. After the water had slowly evaporated, the silica remained. Some of the silica precipitated as uniformly sized and aligned spheres, which agglomerated into opal. Opal in the shape of plants or animals of a past geologic age are opal fossils.

Opal fossils and regular opal formed simultaneously, often near each other. Chemically they are the same. The only difference between them is where they formed. If an opal formed in pockets, cracks, or fissures in rock, ironstone, or sandstone, it is simply an opal, not a fossil.

For some still unexplained reason, a high percentage of fossils are very fine quality opal. When miners find an outstanding specimen that has the potential of being cut into dozens of gems, they make an economic judgement as to which will fetch more money, polished cabochons or fossils; most of the time gem use wins. Because of its value as

Umoona Opal Mine & Museum

gemstones, most fossil opal no longer exists as an identifiable biological form. Generally, only unusual examples remain. Sometimes there is a compromise, as with the snail-shaped crystal opals, found in Shellpatch at Coober Pedy (above right). Instead of leaving them as recognizable fossils, or cabbing them, the owner sculpted them into shapes reminiscent of the sea.

Cigar-shaped opal pipes could have come from cephalopod shells, spaces within rocks, or even tree limbs. Without individual cell details, they are likely void replacements. In contrast, visible growth rings in the Cretaceous Period wood slice (see page 45) indicate the wood was only partially opalized.

Umoona Opal Mine & Museum

43

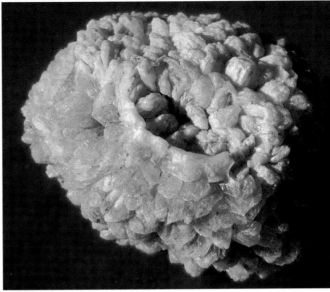

Sheep shearer and miner Theodore Matthey uncovered this magnificent opal "pineapple" in 1903. His deathbed wish saved it from going the way of all but a few others—being broken up for gems. He asked that it be preserved to show to his grandchildren. Opal pineapples are pseudo-morphs, opal replacements of what was once believed to have been the mineral glauberite. New research suggests they may have been ikalite, first replaced by calcite, then by opal.

Rough Times

*P*ineapples, so named because of their shape, are pseudomorphs (literally, *false form*), objects that have taken the shape of other objects. Originally, pseudomorphs were defined as minerals that took the crystalline form of another mineral. Scientists have since relaxed the definition somewhat to accommodate almost any object's taking the shape of another. In pineapples, opal replaced not a living organism but mineral crystals. For years mineralogists thought the opal had supplanted a cluster of glauberite. Now some researchers believe the original crystals were ikalite, which were replaced by calcite, which was finally replaced by opal. No matter the sequence, the result is a precious collectible opal object.

Opal pineapples were found before the original opal mine at White Cliffs was commercialized. Rarer than flawless diamonds, they have become, with dinosaur bones, the most important and valuable opalized objects. No mine besides White Cliffs has ever produced them; and estimates are that after more than a century, only a few hundred have ever been recovered. Almost all of the opal pineapples are now gone, having been cut into gemstones because miners could get more money for many opal cabochons than they could for one pseudomorph.

Some opalized fossils look almost too real to be believed. They are natural "copies." Both these Australian specimens are jawbones from Cretaceous monotremes, egg-laying mammals (**Steropodon galmani,** *top;* **Kollikodon ritchiei,** *bottom*). *They are replacement products, opalized jawbones in the shape of the originals. Beyond curiosities, such fossils are national scientific treasures.*

The Australian Museum
(both)

44

Occasionally an entirely new opal object comes to light. In 1990 the gem trade first saw cat's-eye opal from Brazil. A fibrous material often with dendritic inclusions, these opals are likely pseudomorphs, opal replacements, of a still unknown substance.

Smithsonian Institution

Fossils involving opal show two distinct structures, indicating they formed by two slightly different processes. Some became solid opal, proof that voids in the shape of organisms or remnants of organisms, such as mollusks, crustaceans, bones, and tree limbs, had filled with silica and water. Partially-opalized fossils, including many recovered dinosaur bones, wood, and seashells, retain the original shape but only some of the host material. Even though they are not solid opal, often they display exquisite detail and vivid color.

The wood slice below, recovered at Duck Creek, Queensland, looks realistic millions of years after it was part of a living tree. Its annual growth rings and bark are mineralized as a cellular mirror of the original, while its core is opalized. The jawbones (opposite) are opalized, but the teeth contain the original enamel.

Some opalized objects seem to be plentiful. For instance, large numbers of snails, pipes, and dinosaur bones regularly appear on the market. Shellpatch at Coober Pedy and several areas at Andamooka probably contained the world's greatest concentrations of opal fossils and opalized marine creatures. Opal pipes are intriguing because each Australian mining area has a different explanation for the usually stubby, cigar-shaped opals. In South Australia they are said to be replacement products of extinct shellfish related to squids, cuttlefish and octopi. Queensland miners believe they are mainly replacements of small tree limbs. Any cylindrical void could have produced them.

The Australian Museum

Looking at opal fossils gives me the feeling that nature has bestowed a double gift—a tangible timeline and a gem. Although millions of years lie between sequences, past and present combine here in my hand. Nature has modernized ancient history in a sumptuous way. Nothing is quite so tantalizing as a large opal fossil. Though I would not want to cut it, I would like nothing more than to know what gems it might contain.

Two recent events illustrate how much pride Australians take in their opal. In 1993 the government officially proclaimed opal the National Gemstone of Australia. Then, in 1995 two holographic postage stamps acknowledged the honor; this one for light opal, and one for black opal on page 19.

MEXICAN
OPAL

M exico is so famous as the main source for one particular type opal that *Mexican* is almost always included in its name. Few other countries and gems are as intimately linked in history and in the minds of the world's gem-buying public. For instance, not many consumers are familiar with Russian diamonds, Sri Lankan sapphires, or Canadian jade. But such pairings of well-known sources and their main products do exist in a few cases: Burma rubies, Colombian emeralds—and Mexican opals.

Other nations, including the USA, mine brown, red, yellow, and orange opal without play-of-color. But not like Mexico's. When gems burn like glowing embers, bright and vibrant as those featured on the opposite page, they are almost always volcanically-formed Mexican opal. Their body color makes them special enough to have their own name, *Mexican fire opal*.

These lively, popular stones are defined, not on the basis of body tone, the gradient for Australian opal, but body color. Mexican opal has warm body colors—yellowish orange to reddish brown—with or without play-of-color. When such yellow, orange, or red opal also shows play-of-color, it has its own name, *precious Mexican fire opal*.

Once Spain had conquered the Americas in the early 1500s, Europe saw the first quantities of opal different from its customary Hungarian stones. Of course, at that time no countries as such existed in Central and South America. The Spanish dealt with natives they called *Indians* in three powerful city states, the Aztecs in central Mexico, the Maya in southern Mexico, Guatemala, and Honduras, and the Incas in Peru. Although no one knows how early opal use began, all three cultures mined and treasured opal.

Fortunately, a few examples of those historic opals remain. Probably the best known was once named the *Hope Opal*, cataloged in 1839 and named for its famous collector-owner, who also owned the *Hope Diamond*. Definitely atypical of today's Mexican opal, the inch-long, 35-carat gem, now called the

As wildly colorful as flames, even without opal's typical play-of-color, Mexican fire opal seems to express its volcanic origin in pulsing high-chroma reds, oranges, yellows, and browns. Semi-transparent to translucent, these gemstones are usually faceted to heighten their impact.

Precious Mexican fire opal, *fire opal with play-of-color, commands the highest prices of Mexico's gems (above). Red, yellow, green, and blue flashes appear to dance in liquid as the stones turn. When sufficiently transparent to read through, they may also be called* crystal opal. *Except for fire opal, most other Mexican opal is cut as cabochons to emphasize color.*

Other transparent Mexican opal, usually but not necessarily colorless and with little or no color play, is jelly, *or* water *opal (left).*

Genex, NY (both)

Aztec Sun God Opal (see page 2), is transparent blue with play-of-color. Another fairly well-documented opal, the 32-carat *El Aguila Azteca* (the *Aztec Eagle*), may have belonged to both Moctezuma and Emperor Maximilian. The head of the Mexican revolutionary forces gave it to American Herbert J. Browne in 1914 for his help in supplying arms and ammunition, but its location today is unknown.

Other gems used by the native cultures have been lost in time and circumstance as they moved without documentation from conquered chiefs to local gentry or back to European courts. In a Velasquez portrait done about 1692, the subject, a male secretary to the Governor of New Mexico, wears an identifiable fire opal from Zimapan, most likely a pre-Columbian piece. Just as happened with Guatemalan jadeite, Mexican opal mining apparently ceased once the Spanish destroyed the indigenous cultures. Therefore, Aztecs probably mined opal in use between 1519, when Cortés arrived, and the mid-1800s, when Querétaro's deposits were rediscovered.

The first new opal mine to open was Santa Maria del Iris, in 1870. In the next two decades the area around Querétaro, which is both a city and a state about 200km northwest of Mexico City, supported more than a hundred separate mines. Today only a few remain active even though the historic colonial town has grown to half a million people. The region is rich in opal, both in quantity and variety. Wolf Kuehn, of the Canadian Institute of Gemology, recently noticed that some of the volcanic rock used to construct downtown buildings and village houses exhibits visible traces of opal. Production from just a few square meters can include fire opal, precious fire opal, crystals, and gems of half a dozen separate colors.

Mining methods have changed little over the last century. Workers still dig open-pit quarries by hand. They search for opal that formed in pink-to-red rhyolite lava flows after silica-rich groundwater had filled gas cavities. In contrast to Australia, where almost all precious opal appears in sedimentary deposits, in Mexico, Central and South America (except in Brazil), as well as in Nevada, Oregon, and Idaho in the USA, commercial opals formed in volcanic deposits.

Today Mexican opal production is steady, although it is increasingly difficult to find workers willing to do such hard physical labor for low pay. Opal occurs in nine other Mexican states, but activity continues to center around Querétaro, which leads in quality and volume. Years ago most finishing was done in town, where cutters domed all stones into cabochons, including fire opal. Now most fire opal is faceted and most crystal, jelly, and water opal is cabbed. Around 1994, QVC, the television mass-marketer, attempted without success to give opal a new look by offering small faceted jelly opals and pale fire opals.

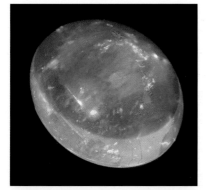

Because of Mexican superstition and the bad-luck legacy that plagues opal, there is little domestic demand for opal. Fortunately, there is a brisk global demand that brings overseas buyers who bargain for rough, transporting it to Hong Kong, Japan, the USA, and Germany.

To the Mexican opal varieties we have seen thus far, add another, *Mexican matrix opal*. You recall that Mexico's volcanic opal forms inside a rhyolite lava flow. Just as Australia's boulder opal is cut to retain some of the ironstone matrix in which it formed, so too is Mexican opal often cut with portions of rhyolite matrix attached.

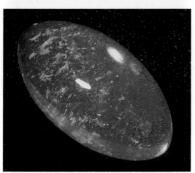

Some of Mexico's variety is evident in this opal trio. The top and bottom gems, with their delicate play-of-color, are transparent enough for reading through; therefore, they are called **crystal opal.** *The center example is* **precious Mexican fire opal** *because of its warm body color and the presence of play-of-color.*

Mexican matrix opal (unlike Australia's ironstone matrix boulder opal, pages 28-29), forms in a pink, cream, tan, or brick-red rhyolite matrix. Of volcanic origin, these baroque three-dimensional opals surrounded by matrix offer substantial mass. When the rhyolite is partially cut away to reveal the opal, the contrast of matrix and opal creates a look popular with both jewelry designers and stone carvers.

Genex, NY (all)

The effect can be stunning, with fire opal or precious opal peeking through a layer of red, cream, pink, or tan rhyolite (above and below). Obviously, the rhyolite can be cut away, but increasingly, designers realize the creative potential of free-form shapes flashing with attention-getting colors. Depending on its dimensions and how much opal is exposed, a stone can either be trimmed by hand (as in the red piece above) or tumbled.

Tucson '96, the huge annual February gem show, introduced one more Mexican opal type to the public (opposite). Like its namesake, leopard opal does indeed have spots. It was formed in a black vesicular basalt whose vesicles filled with light opal. In the dappled leopard opal, the play-of-color appears to dart from spot to spot.

As attractive and relatively inexpensive as Mexican opal is, a perceived and actual problem with the material dampens its acceptance. Once it is removed from the ground, volcanic opal has a tendency to crack and craze more often than opal from sedimentary deposits. Also, some material fades when it is exposed to daylight. Such problems with Mexican opal may be overstated. Still, the question of durability has plagued Mexican opal since its reintroduction into the market last century.

Querétaro mine operators used to spread their newly-mined material on their roofs to dry for a couple of months to make sure they only sold stable opal. Apparently that practice no longer exists. Miners have passed the responsibility now to dealers. Several reliable wholesalers do hold Mexican

opal two to three months before selling it and offer to replace opals that craze within a reasonable time period.

To see a volcanic opal deposit and get the facts on eastern Oregon's mountainside opal mine. As we cracked opened "thunder eggs" (rhyolite spheres) with sledge hammers, I saw about half the newly-exposed opal craze within half an hour (see page 40). No one has ever found a way to stop some opal from cracking when it is initially exposed to air. Miners agree it is best to leave material that is going to craze at the mine, instead of transporting it to town before separating it from stable material.

Martin Fuller collection

Generally, if an opal out of the ground remains uncrazed after three months in the air, chances are good it is stable enough to be used in jewelry. Obviously, there are some exceptions. Extreme conditions will endanger most opal and severely test the three-month rule, such as heating newly mined material, leaving it in the sun, or transporting it to a desert climate.

We have all seen dealers at gem shows selling Mexican opal housed in bottles or tubes filled with water. Although wetting opal does make the colors look intense, some buyers are confused by the practice, believing Mexican opal has to remain submerged to be safe. That is not true. Some opal will craze even in water. Some will never craze. Many Mexican opals remain intact after centuries of use. Stability depends on how the opal was formed and how much water it maintains. Unfortunately for a buyer, there is no simple test. From the same mine two opals that look similar may react entirely differently when worn as jewelry.

Even experts can be surprised. When I recently photographed one of the most famous opal collections in the world, I saw material that had not been crazed when it had entered the collection a few years ago. After being displayed under hot museum lights for a relatively short time, some fine specimens are now badly damaged. As the opals had been worn more than fifty years, the staff had assumed they were stable and safe from cracking.

Opal with a lower water content, and thus weighing less because of its lower specific gravity, is less likely to craze than opal with more water. There is no easy test to determine which opal may crack or craze in time. Proper care coupled with avoiding temperature and humidity extremes are the best precautions.

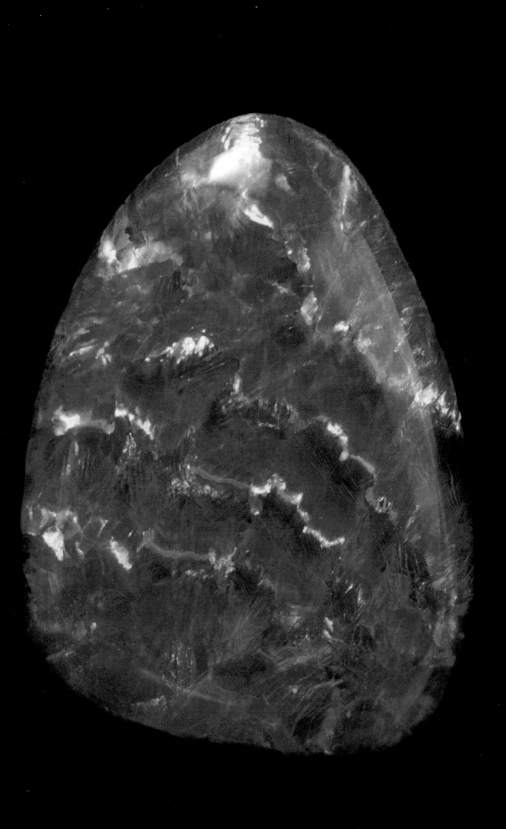

ASSEMBLED OPALS, SYNTHETICS, & SIMULANTS

Synthetic opal is laboratory produced with the same chemistry as natural opal. Today's markets contain many other gem synthetics, including rubies, sapphires, emeralds, amethyst, and even diamonds. Opal simulants are any non-opal materials made to look like opal, such as glass or plastic.

Several opal and opal-related products combine natural opal with other materials: doublets, which contain a slice of natural opal glued to potch, glass, or other base material; and triplets, which contain the base plus a slice of opal plus a crystal or glass top. Known as *assembled opal* because people put the parts together, they are not to be confused with natural opal.

Naturals are usually found in seams, often with precious opal atop a layer of potch or common opal, sometimes with precious opal sandwiched between two potch layers. If a cutter leaves some potch on the bottom of a light or black opal, the opal is not considered a doublet. But if someone glues a potch base to a piece of precious opal, the result is a doublet. The difference is whether nature connects opal and potch or a human joins them with glue. Doublets are still available, but triplets dominate the less expensive end of the opal market. Triplets used to be assembled with quartz tops, opal centers, and potch bottoms. On the next page you will see how they are made today.

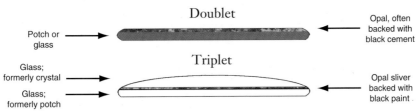

Doublet

Potch or glass →
← Opal, often backed with black cement

Triplet

Glass; formerly crystal →
Glass; formerly potch →
← Opal sliver backed with black paint

Assembled opals contain less opal than they appear to. Doublets have two parts, opal and a glass or potch backing, which are joined together with black cement. Triplets have a glass top, a sliver of opal (painted black on one side) and a glass backing. Only a few years ago triplets contained a quartz dome, an opal layer, and a black potch backing (opposite).

E. Gregory Sherman, Pty. Ltd. (opposite)

The Making of a Modern Opal Triplet

Triplets provide customers with an opal look at costume jewelry prices. They let miners use both gem-quality opal and material too thin or "cracky" to sell as gems.

In minutes, 210 reciprocating parallel metal blades, bathed in an abrasive corundum slurry, slice opals into ultra-thin slivers. Toothed saw blades would destroy material this fragile.

The paper-thin opal slivers, only 0.006 inches thick, flex in a hand. Almost transparent, they need an opaque black backing to emphasize their play-of-color.

H & K Blopel Opal Cutter, Coober Pedy (all)

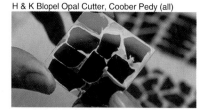

Spray-painting the transparent opal slivers black on one side creates the impression of a black opal. Assembly of an opal triplet begins with gluing the black side onto a glass plate.

Seen from the top, the light opal slivers play their colors against the background of black spray paint. Next pre-cut glass domes are glued directly onto the top of each opal.

Each domed assemblage is cut away from the glass plate. The edges are ground to finish the process. Each triplet (below) comprises a glass base, black paint backing an opal sliver, and a glass top.

Doublets are a means to produce a wearable gem from opal too thin to be used alone. In this early example, the opal is glued onto a base of gray potch.

E. Gregory Sherman, Pty. Ltd. (3)

This doublet has a thinner opal layer than the one above and a thicker potch base. Doublets cost considerably less than solid opals.

Even though it has about the same amount of opal as a new one, this old triplet is more substantial because of its domed quartz top and thick potch base. Quartz tops are both harder and tougher than glass.

A ssembled opal offers affordable alternatives to solid opal. Think of doublets and triplets as costume jewelry instead of as investment stones. Doublets were first made in Australia in 1946 and triplets around 1960. They put together a saleable product from opal material not thick enough and perhaps not durable enough to be mounted alone. "Cracky" opal, material prone to crazing, works well in triplets once it is safely enclosed between glass and glue. There is nothing inherently wrong with assembled opal, as long as its construction is disclosed to the buyer at the time of sale.

Whereas glass backs are standard on almost all new assembled opal, note the use of potch as the base in the fifteen- to twenty-year-old examples above. Contemporary triplets can be surprisingly attractive (opposite, bottom). Instead of utilizing a dark potch background to enhance play-of-color and a quartz dome to provide durability, they are glass sandwiches with only black spray paint for contrast. Doublets and triplets require cautious care. They should not be immersed in water lest the parts separate. Also, as new triplets are almost all glass, they may chip and break should you accidentally hit or drop them. Quartz domes, which are almost never used today, were both harder and tougher than new glass domes.

A new Australian product is confounding governments, trade associations, and jewelers, who are unsure how to accurately describe items like this ring. Its thin opal pieces are not backed with the usual glued potch or black paint. Instead, they are set into channels cut into gold and painted black, letting the ring itself serve as a dark background. Some Australian dealers call them *mosaics*, or even *doublets*. They probably should be referred to as *inlays*. No matter how they are described, note how they are made before you buy.

Created by Gilson before the factory moved from Switzerland to Japan, these synthetics deliberately mimic natural opal in type and colors, almost as many as nature produces. The visibly distinctive lizard-skin pattern of their silica spheres (photomicrograph below, 60x) makes identification relatively simple.

Gilson Created Opals from Chatham Created Gems

Synthetic opal is created with the same chemical properties as naturals. Once the underlying structure and cause of color play had been understood (see pages 62-63), people began making opal. Pierre Gilson in France was first, in 1974. Later Kyocera's Inamori gem division introduced its synthetic opal in 1980. Then, a Japanese chemical firm bought the rights to the Gilson name and process. Now the two Japanese companies compete for the relatively small synthetic opal market. A few Russian labs recently tried to make opal, but their output was unsaleable.

Although some of the synthesis process remains secret, both Japanese firms use three similar steps. First, they create silica spheres by evenly distributing a fine silica compound in a water and alcohol solution; then they add an alkali, such as ammonia, to start the reaction. Obviously, companies

like Inamori and Gilson, working in laboratory conditions, precipitate their spheres in tall clean cylinders. As the spheres settle, they naturally align in tightly-packed layers, but soft wet spheres are unsuitable for gems. The challenging final compacting, drying, and hardening step seems to be the one that keeps other firms from succeeding. (Well-known Lightning Ridge opal writer and backyard chemist Len Cram precipitates spheres in cola bottles and peanut butter jars. He says he gets seam opal in only three months using nothing more than opal dirt from a mine, water, and an electrolyte!)

When they deal with any synthetic, gemologists and the gem trade need procedures to separate naturals from laboratory-grown material. A microscopic exam usually suffices for identification, except for lighter-colored synthetic opal, which is often difficult to detect. Because of the laboratory production process, silica spheres collect in columns, which may be evident from the side of a cut gem. A collumnar effect may also appear in some naturals. When viewed from top or bottom, colored spots in synthetic opal display a distinctive "lizard-skin" pattern (above right), which is not seen in naturals.

In 1987 the GIA tested several samples of Inamori's opal. It noted that one characteristic of natural opal is the presence of microscopic amounts of water between the silica spheres. Detecting no water in the Inamori material, GIA proposed that they be called *opal simulants* because their chemistry does not precisely match natural opal. Some gem dealers noted that Colombian emeralds usually contain water, whereas Chatham' flux-grown emeralds do not, even though the gem trade and the government continue to recognize Chatham's created emeralds as synthetics.

Enhancements abound to improve color, disguise cracks, make opals shine, and perhaps even prevent crazing. Many fast, inexpensive surface treatments used on other gems, such as oiling, waxing, heating, dyeing, and filling with resins and plastics, are also attempted with opal. Some experimenters are trying to prevent opals from crazing by waterproofing their surfaces to retain any existing or reintroduced water. The newest enhancements to alter opal colors usually include impregnation with dyed liquid plastic.

Oils, waxes, or polymers forced inside opals with heat and pressure are more controversial than faster, less expensive, and easier to detect surface treatments. As is also the case with the new treated *B* jadeite from Asia, which has been boiled in acid, bleached, filled, and dyed, the only definitive detection for impregnated polymers is expensive infrared spectroscopy.

In an attempt to increase value, two old enhancements turn light opal dark (see page 39). Porous light opal is soaked in a sugar solution, then bathed in sulfuric acid, which darkens the sugar. To detect sugar treatment, use magnification to look for a "peppery" black appearance. A similar blackening effect comes from baking opal in a brown bag or in manure. Smoke and ashes darken the outside of a stone. Use magnification to detect a "flaky" surface.

Simulants, or imitations, are anything made to look like opal. Several opal imitations satisfy the costume jewelry market segment. Common simulants are glass and plastic, but human imagination quickly augments any existing list. People fill glass and plastic domes with colored pieces of wire, plastic, and glass, all in an attempt to suggest opal's play-of-color. There are new stones made of ground opal mixed with epoxy or plastic and formed to look like gems. And one imitation actually is well enough known to be recognized by its brand name.

For two decades Michigan's John Slocum has made and sold "Slocum Stone," a glass imitation opal (above, and right magnified 3x). Choosing not to disclose how he gets color into his layered and flecked material, he tells me he will not patent the process and thus reveal his secret. John says he can produce up to a million carats a year. He thinks someday his process may be more famous as a method of sealing opal cracks than as a method of creating imitation opal.

Opal assembled stones, synthetics, enhancements, treatments, and simulants—all are acceptable to the trade and to the public as long as they are disclosed. What is unfair, unethical, and illegal is to sell such treated or created material as natural. Only natural gems have intrinsic value.

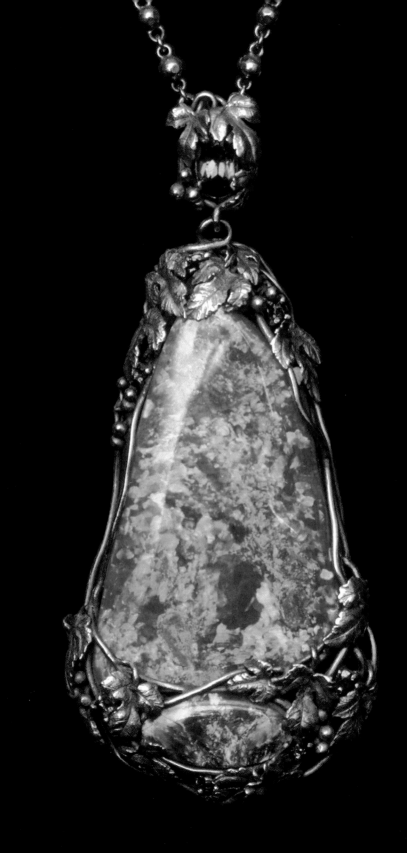

BUYING AND CARING

Buying opal has never been easier—or more expensive. The choices are the widest ever. Recent public awareness and consumer enthusiasm for black opal and boulder opal have caused prices to soar. To accurately assess cost, you need to relate prices to value at the time. In this book I have alluded to individual black and boulder gems of $25,000 to $500,000. If you take government numbers that suggest the average household head in the USA makes about $25,000 a year, then the bag of boulder opal Tully Wollaston bought in 1889 for £27 would cost $12,500 now, and the single boulder opal that sold in London in 1873 for £150 would fetch $75,000 in today's market. Tully risked a great deal of money on his intuition about Australian opal, which international buyers had only glimpsed and for which there was, as yet, no market. He bet right that high quality gems will always bring a high price because they will always be rare and in demand.

On a per-carat basis, fine quality opal generally costs less than the four major crystal gems. Customers in the USA spending more than $1000 usually buy diamonds, emeralds, rubies, and sapphires. Their attitude that opal is an inexpensive gem, not an alternative to the big four, is largely responsible for USA dealers' importing mainly three types of opal: Small calibrated light (most often white) cabochons with little play-of-color; doublets; and triplets. Opal may be sold by the carat or by the piece. The vast majority of opal buyers usually are not shopping at the high end of the market. Indeed, they may not even be aware a high-end opal market exists. Almost all the best black opal goes to Japan and other Asian countries.

The highest prices you will see, thousands to tens of thousands of dollars apiece, will be for black opal, boulder opal, and large, colorful light opal specimens. Sometimes people refer to them as *museum quality*. I prefer to describe them as rare, valuable, beautiful, unique gemstones. And I hope, as additional buyers admire and understand opal, they will add opal to their fine jewelry collections.

Signed "Tiffany & Co." and made around 1910, this gorgeous pendant proves that high-quality opal can last without cracking or crazing. The intricate handmade gold setting includes two Lightning Ridge black opals, five Russian demantoid garnets, and five Montana blue sapphires.

Smithsonian Institution

Beads are among the many objects made from boulder opal matrix, the host material for boulder opal. Seldom sold in stores for what they really are, matrix beads can be extremely attractive and expensive if a good percentage of opal shows.

Mexican opal and the volcanic material from other countries around the world are colorful and usually reasonably priced. Quite attractive fire opal in small sizes is available cut and polished for $100 or less, unmounted. Expect to pay $1000 or more for larger, brighter pieces.

Assembled opal costs considerably less than comparable solid opal. Triplets cost the least of any opal product, as they contain only a sliver of opal. Make sure you are getting what you pay for. On a limited budget, you can enjoy the look of opal by buying doublets and triplets. But do not let anyone tell you they are "solid" opal.

To buy an opal, decide what size and color you want and how much you want to spend. Advertisements in your Sunday newspaper, in mail order catalogs, and on TV shopping channels may lead you to believe all opal is insipid light or white with little play-of-color. Almost any jewelry store will have the least expensive opal—doublets, triplets, and small almost colorless white cabs, each of which fills a market niche.

You can usually find an opal for $100 or less, unmounted, in most local jewelry stores. If you want higher quality, you can almost always special order what you desire. You do not have to buy gems sight-unseen. If you want a $1000 to $2000 gem, your retailer can consign goods from an opal wholesaler to make an excellent selection of stones available to you. To obtain an extraordinary gem, most likely you or your jeweler will need to contact an opal specialist, who has access to the finest material.

Looking at the photographs in this book, you see how beautiful opal can be, and many antique jewels attest to its durability. Opal has versatility to combine with other gemstones. It changes character with every shift of light, offering effects of imagination, refinement, subtlety, and verve. Opal is equally appropriate for a business or dressy occasion. Its dramatic color range compliments almost any outfit and suits any mood.

Named the Kaleidoscope by its owner, this lovely blue-green black opal pendant is from Lightning Ridge. Black opal does not seem to craze as often as light or volcanic opal, a reality attributed to its water content, potch backing, and thicker cuts. Nevertheless, black opal requires proper care too.

This cameo is assembled from a thin machine-carved opal portrait and a black onyx base. It requires care in cleaning not only because of the opal but also because of the glue. Such cameos should not be soaked in water, subjected to heat or chemicals, or placed in ultrasonic or steam cleaners.

E. Gregory Sherman, Pty. Ltd.

Caring for opal should be a routine event. Softer than the most popular crystal gemstones and naturally containing water, opal requires special considerations. On the Mohs hardness scale of 1-10, diamonds (the hardest of all materials) are 10, talc is 1, and quartz is 7. Because it is so common in our environment, quartz is often used as a hardness standard. Any gem harder than 7 will not be scratched when it rubs against most rocks, car doors, steel sinks, ceramic counters, and other everyday items. Such everyday items as steel, stone walls, tiles, quartz, and gems like amethyst, spinel, emeralds, rubies, sapphires, and diamonds can scratch opal, which on the Mohs scale is 5 - 6 ½. Store each piece of your opal jewelry in its own padded cloth bag. Any gem will break with certain direct hits. Because of their structure, opals are particularly vulnerable.

Water affects assembled opal and solid opal differently. Remove a doublet or a triplet ring from your finger before washing your hands or bathing. The glue reacts to prolonged exposure to water, dulling the appearance of the assembled stone as the layers separate. To clean all opal products, avoid ultrasonic cleaners and steamers, bleach, all chemicals, and cleaners. You can safely wash solid opal jewelry in plain warm water or soapy water (no detergent). Oil will discolor your opal. Neither oiling nor storing opal in water prevents cracking or heals existing cracks.

Opal dehydrates soon after being mined, then stabilizes. Most opal that has survived for several months without crazing is likely to stay intact. But do not expose opal to high heat, direct sun, bright and hot showcase lights, desert conditions, low humidity bank vaults, and similar temperature and humidity extremes. Rapid thermal changes also jeopardize the stability of your opal. Remove your opal ring while you are cooking. Wear gloves when departing a cozy 75°F living room for a sub-zero winter outing. With reasonable care, your opal treasure will long provide you elegant beauty.

Quality opal beads are rare and therefore expensive. Large pieces of precious opal that have been carved, such as **The Fan,** *a brooch with carved black opal, are also unusual and precious. To avoid surface damage and cracking, treat opal gently, as gems.*

E. Gregory Sherman, Pty. Ltd.

Karen Lindley Pty. Ltd.

P lay-of-color in opal depends on several factors: Silica sphere diameter, sphere uniformity and alignment, angle of incident light, viewer angle, and orientation of the stone. Electron and scanning-electron microscopes in the 1960s first revealed that microscopic silica spheres with water interspersed among them make up opal ($SiO_2 \cdot nH_2O$). Light striking these spheres, each only 150 to 300 nanometers in diameter, diffracts, or bends slightly. The interference caused by light waves overlapping reinforces some colors and cancels others. Thus, a combination of *diffraction* and *interference* causes opal colors. With spheres larger than 300 nanometers or smaller than 150 nanometers or irregular in size, shape, or alignment, we see scrambled black or white light and call such opal *potch*. In the stone orientation sequence opposite, see how colors shift with four 90° rotations of the same opal, making it look like different gems. Changing the orientation of the viewer also affects what colors are perceived.

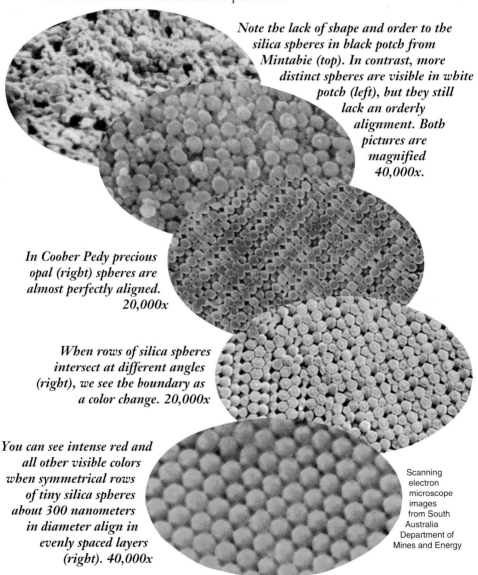

Note the lack of shape and order to the silica spheres in black potch from Mintabie (top). In contrast, more distinct spheres are visible in white potch (left), but they still lack an orderly alignment. Both pictures are magnified 40,000x.

In Coober Pedy precious opal (right) spheres are almost perfectly aligned. 20,000x

When rows of silica spheres intersect at different angles (right), we see the boundary as a color change. 20,000x

You can see intense red and all other visible colors when symmetrical rows of tiny silica spheres about 300 nanometers in diameter align in evenly spaced layers (right). 40,000x

Scanning electron microscope images from South Australia Department of Mines and Energy

62

To show shifts in color play, the same opal was turned 90° for each view, while holding camera angle and light source constant.

George Brooks & Schorr Marketing

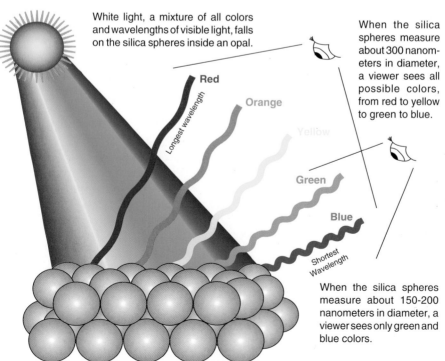

White light, a mixture of all colors and wavelengths of visible light, falls on the silica spheres inside an opal.

Red

Longest wavelength

Orange

Yellow

Green

Blue

Shortest Wavelength

When the silica spheres measure about 300 nanometers in diameter, a viewer sees all possible colors, from red to yellow to green to blue.

When the silica spheres measure about 150-200 nanometers in diameter, a viewer sees only green and blue colors.

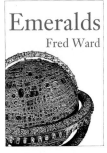

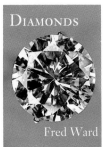

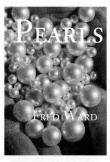

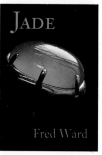

About Fred Ward
and his Gem Book Series

Fred Ward at Lightning Ridge, Australia

Glamour, intrigue, romance, the quest for treasure... those are all vital aspects of humankind's eternal search and love for gemstones. As long as people have roamed the world, they have placed extraordinary value on our incredible gifts from the land and sea.

Opals is the seventh in a series of gem books written and photographed by Fred Ward. Each book, *Rubies & Sapphires, Emeralds, Diamonds, Pearls, Gem Care, Jade,* and *Opals,* is part of a twenty-year global search into the history, geology, lore, and sources of these priceless treasures. He personally has visited the sites and artifacts displayed here to provide the most authentic and timely information available in the field. Fred Ward's original articles on all these topics except opals first appeared in *National Geographic* Magazine. In addition to being a journalist, Mr. Ward is a Graduate Gemologist (GIA), the highest academic achievement in the gem trade.

Mr. Ward, a respected authority on gems and gemology, is in great demand as a speaker to professional and private groups. He and designer Carol Tutera own Blue Planet Gems, Inc., a custom jewelry studio. *Opals* was designed using PageMaker 6.01 layouts on a Power Computing Powertower Pro 225MHz computer and printed by H & D Graphics using Adobe Janson typefaces.